Eva-Marie Kröller

George Bowering:
Bright Circles of Colour

Talonbooks · Vancouver · 1992

© 1992 The Author

TALONBOOKS
201 – 1019 East Cordova
Vancouver, British Columbia V6A 1M8
Canada

Published with assistance from the Canada Council
Designed and typeset at Coach House Printing, Toronto

Printed and bound in Canada by Hignell Printing Limited

CANADIAN CATALOGUING IN PUBLICATION DATA
Kroeller, Eva-Marie.
George Bowering.
(Talonbooks' new Canadian criticism series)
Includes bibliographical references and index.
ISBN 0-88922-306-8
1. Bowering, George, 1935- . Criticism and interpretation.
I. Title. II. Series.
PS8503.O875Z736 1992   C811'.54   C92-091067-X
PR9199.3B69Z736 1992

Acknowledgements

Much of the material for this study was collected in the Fine Arts Library of the University of British Columbia, the library of the Vancouver Art Gallery, and the National Gallery of Canada, and my thanks go to the librarians and archivists who assisted me there. Laurie Ricou and Peter Quartermain offered helpful bibliographical and critical advice; Roy Kiyooka showed me the original collages for *The Man in Yellow Boots;* Greg Curnoe answered questions about his Dorval mural; Christoph Irmscher shared his ideas on William Carlos Williams with me; Frank Davey, Laurie Ricou, Susan Knutson, Martin Kuester, Richard Cavell, and Thomas Hastings permitted me to see unpublished work, and Smaro Kamboureli and Robert Kroetsch gave me permission to quote from a personal letter. Helpful criticism came from Karl Siegler and Frank Davey. Above all, George Bowering provided answers, and additional puzzlement, to my many questions. One chapter contains adapted versions of essays previously published in the *University of Ottawa Quarterly* and *Open Letter;* my thanks to their editors for allowing me to reprint them here. Louise Owen, Julie Walchli, and Susanne Goodison were exemplary research assistants, and the students of my 1989 graduate seminar gave me an opportunity to put the ideas presented here to the test. Funding was provided by a research grant of the University of British Columbia. This book has been published with the help of a grant from the Canadian Federation for the Humanities, using funds provided by the Social Sciences and Humanities Research Council of Canada.

Bright Circles of Colour is offered as a tribute to Ann Munton, who taught me much about Canadian poetry and even more about dignity and courage.

In memory of Ann Munton
1948-1990

Contents

Acknowledgements 7

Introduction 9

ONE   A Community of Correspondences: TISH 13

TWO   Cubist Collage: *The Man in Yellow Boots* 27

THREE   Newspaper Collage: *Rocky Mountain Foot* 40

FOUR   Bowering and the London Scene 51

FIVE   Montreal, Guido Molinari and the *Kerrisdale Elegies* 71

SIX   The *Burning Water* Trilogy 84

SEVEN   The Making of a Literary Reputation 112

Notes 123

Works by George Bowering 125

Works Cited 128

Index 137

Introduction

In 1979, George Bowering dedicated his collection of poems *Another Mouth* "to three artists who have graced my life, illuminated my imagination, & talkt my ear off: Greg Curnoe, Roy Kiyooka, & Brian Fisher." At first sight, nothing could be more dissimilar than Curnoe's militant regionalism and gaudy Pop Art creations on the one hand, and the formal restraint and urbane allure of Fisher and Kiyooka's Hard Edge work on the other. Questioned about the sources of his art, Curnoe responded with a list of his favourite comic book heroes and the seemingly casual statement "I see things and some things stay with me" (Curnoe 42). Fisher and Kiyooka, by contrast, offered philosophical, even rhapsodic, pronouncements in keeping with the universalist vocabulary of their work: "And someday i would like to build a gate – a huge gate, one that hallows the ground where the sea and the land conjoin to make a passageway to the house of sky.... Art aint anything without the sacred" (*Kiyooka* n.p.), and "[Man] stands alone in unhappy isolation. He must come to a greater awareness of present timespace through a realization of his own vital involvement.... The meaning of any work of art is its shared human experience" (Fisher 48). Bowering's dedication of his book to painters as diverse as these appears to confirm the irreconcilable contradiction observed time and again in his work by reviewers, who have alternately scolded him for being too cerebral and too banal. Thus critics have taken issue with his "terribly skilful, almost masterful work" (Bergé 10),[1] suggesting that he has closed himself off from authentic experience, or they have complained that his "poetry is on the verge of turning into poetics, perception into epistemology" (Wilson 362), while others object that "many of his experiences are in themselves intrinsically commonplace: sex, death, and menstruation are data, like rain" (Harrison 75). To his most persistent critic, Robin Mathews, such contradiction proves an insincerity which disqualifies Bowering as a socially relevant author (Mathews 1982/83: 31-32).

Yet such insincerity can only be postulated if the everyday and the universal are indeed mutually exclusive or if one is deceitfully used to mask the other. Instead of demanding that Bowering commit himself to one position only, critics and fellow-writers like Robin Blaser, Smaro Kamboureli and Margaret Atwood understand his work to be derived from a poetics of unrest, "a processional of mind and heart" (Blaser 10).[2] To them, Bowering's many works present a continuous text "where the dynamic can be seen at work, where the displayed persona is at war with the hidden, pained, meditative, authentic self or voice" (Atwood 6). This unrest, which implies an "obsessive need to take hold of nothing" (Spanos 149),[3] is frequently thematized in the figure of the *flâneur* ("The Walking Poem"), the tourist (the Mexican poems and *A Short Sad Book*), the explorer (*Burning Water*), or the "lone ranger" (*Caprice*). Bowering's poems and short stories, "Spans" (*Protective Footwear*) in particular, are full of inconclusive quests, chases and detective work, embodying "George the Picaro, exactly the same at the end of the road as he was at the beginning of it" (Bowering, 1979b: 96).

Bowering was attracted to the work of Kiyooka, Curnoe, and Fisher, because it demonstrated a similar "unrest." Despite their peacefulness and perfection, Fisher and Kiyooka's works are "unquiet canvases," whose openness is suggested in titles such as *Odysee, Indicant,* or *Convergence.* According to Fisher, a pulsing energy involves his *moiré* creations in "the dynamic interrelationships of things, the configurations of energy fields" (Fisher 50). Kiyooka, who has always insisted that the pure geometric forms in his paintings are derived from "prosaic sources" (Macdonald 651), also uses concrete images when he describes his goal as wanting "to lay beside a mountain the fragility of a painting; the fragrance of a life lived" (Macdonald 651). Conversely, a cosmic illumination may emerge from the everyday clutter in Curnoe's paintings: speaking, in *Kerrisdale Elegies,* about the beautiful dead "who sprout flames in the dark before morning," Bowering marvels at their similarity with his friend's creations:

> They turn
> bright circles of colour,
> > like the painted bicycle
> wheels of Greg Curnoe,
> > king child.

All three painters posit a universe where man has relinquished his Cartesian position of privilege and control and patiently sets about to decipher the language of things. The severe geometry in the painters' work does not signify an order and symmetry imposed from the outside, but one which

Introduction

has communicated itself from the phenomena to the viewer: "it is the interior structural configuration which dictates the exterior, unique forms into which phenomena shape themselves" (Fisher 51). This approach is not only opposed to a rationalist analysis of phenomena but also to expressionism, for, although grounded in spontaneous gesture, expressionism still imposes the artist's vision on the world: all three painters are to be understood in sharp contrast to Abstract Expressionism, and Bowering made his own views on the movement known in his comments on Franz Kline who "painted in the hues of statesmen's shoes" (*Uncle Louis*).

The basic "unique forms into which phenomena shape themselves" also dominate Bowering's poetics, which return time and again to the configurations of two parallel lines, two lines crossing each other at right angles and the oval or diamond. Each has its root in the things of his daily life: the mountains and trees of Bowering's childhood in the Okanagan; the field staked out by the positions in his favourite sport, baseball; the edge of water and shore on the west coast. In *Allophanes* (1976), Bowering even includes drawings of his poetic creed: man, his "arms [flung] wide / into the juicy air" (*Kerrisdale Elegies*), is placed within a diamond grid linking him to air, water, fire, and earth. Alluringly simple as these configurations may be, however, they are heavily freighted with rationalist connotations, whether it be the figure-ground constructions of Euclidean geometry or the design of "Vitruvian Man," who – distorted out of natural shape – flings his limbs wide to prove his central position in the cosmos. In order to unsettle such connotations, Bowering, Curnoe and Kiyooka often combine basic geometric configurations with the collage, whose disjunctions correspond to the opacity and independence of things, making "geometry" a true "measuring of the earth." Donald B. Kuspit has called the collage the "organizing principle of art in the age of the relativity of art" and presented rich evidence of its ability to deconstruct hegemonies, definitions, and unities. The question of validity does not arise in collage, Kuspit argues, "because it is an experiment in ordering reality, rather than a way of decisively determining it" (49).

The following will be an exploration of selected works by Bowering and their interdependencies with the visual arts, the collage foremost among them. From his early works, Bowering's affinity with the arts is clearly apparent, whether it be manifested in Gordon Payne's drawings for *Sticks & Stones* (planned to be included in the 1962 Tishbook but only recently published in a Talonbooks edition), Bowering's persistent name-dropping in *Mirror on the Floor* (1967) (e.g. "I saw him in a blurry Goya kind of a way") or poems such as "The Swing," "On a Black Painting by Tamayo" and "Vancouver Étude." More recent works, such as *Burning Water* and *Kerrisdale Elegies*, allude to William Blake and Greg Curnoe. Sometimes, the contact with a specific painter is well-documented, such as Kiyooka and Bowering's collaboration on *The Man in Yellow Boots* (1965) and Curnoe and Bowering's particularly rich partnership. On other occasions, as in Bowering's response to Jack Chambers, Brian Fisher, and Guido Molinari, an interdependence may be less extensively established, but can still be explored as an illuminating parallel. My focus will be on Bowering's responses to contemporary Canadian painters, but there will also be references (in the sections on the *Burning Water* trilogy) to the theories of the British art critic John Berger, with whom Bowering initiated a brief correspondence, and to historical photography. This approach has not been chosen to replace the question of the alleged lack of "social relevance" which so many critics have found troubling in Bowering's work, with anodyne aesthetic concerns. On the contrary, I intend to argue that Bowering's discussion of visual strategies is at the centre of an uncompromising commitment to his art. This commitment does have a moral and social dimension, even if, as Kuspit persuasively argues, its validity must be constantly re-negotiated.

CHAPTER ONE

A Community of Correspondences[1]: TISH

And a couple of days ago I was standing on the pointed end of a B.C. ferry, my real long hair blowing in the sea breeze. Vancouver is a tremendous turn-on town, everywhere you go there are acid-heads, leaning on bridge rails looking at the ocean. Even all the school teachers I know there are acid heads. The professors got long long hair. The radio hit parade plays all day long beautiful psychedelic songs like "It's a turned-on day, and I dig it," and "Come dream with me." Everyone going to Sam Perry's Sound Palace and lying on floor to hear weird music and watch wild color projections on the walls. Once in a while someone gets picked up for pot, but most everyone cool with acid, and there's no way the cops can stop that. In Vancouver you get the notion that the square world no longer has any control of anything.

(George Bowering in a letter to *El Corno Emplumado* 22 [1967])

For someone who has taken pains to convince his biographers of the haphazardness of his life, Bowering has remarkably often been in the right place at the right time – proof, he might argue, of the existence of synchronicities and correspondences. He arrived in Vancouver when it was ready to emerge from its reputation as cultural backwater assigned until then to most Canadian cities outside Montreal and Toronto. Although Vancouver lacked virtually all prerequisites for a "scene" – collectors, galleries, critics, an adequate budget – energetic and courageous individuals conspired to create a rich and lively locale, whose bohemian ambience has best been evoked in Bowering's novel *Mirror on the Floor* (1967) and in Al Neil's autobiographical text, *Changes* (1970). Curators Doris Shadbolt and Tony Emery of the Vancouver Art Gallery and Alvin Balkind of the Fine Arts Gallery at the University of British Columbia, Abraham Rogatnick of the UBC School of Architecture, Douglas Christmas of the Douglas Gallery, and two men who were to be of special importance to Bowering's career, Warren Tallman, professor of English at the University of British Columbia, and Roy Kiyooka, artist and instructor at the Vancouver School of Art, – all these contributed to placing Vancouver on a par with the most important art centres in North America. Like the Emma Lake Workshops in Saskatchewan and the Nova Scotia College of Art and Design under the leadership of Garry Neill Kennedy, the Vancouver scene was strongly oriented towards the United States, distancing itself both from European influences and an increasingly militant Canadian nationalism. For Balkind, the events in Vancouver were "a response to the surge of postwar artistic energy first released by the abstract expressionists in New York," and he described the purpose of exhibitions and happenings as helping "to catalyze and regenerate local artists by putting them in direct touch with the makers of the charged ideas then current largely in New York and California" (Balkind 72). In a similar vein, Philip Leider's essay "Vancouver: Scene with no Scene," published in *ARTSCANADA* in 1967, compared the city's development to that of Los Angeles, San Francisco, and Washington, and one of the few useful documentations of Vancouver's local talent to appear at the time is the catalogue prepared for an exhibition entitled *The New Art of Vancouver* held at the Newport Harbor Art Museum in Balboa, California, in 1969. TISH, the magazine with which Bowering was associated from 1961 until 1963, aggressively refused to be identified with Canadian nationalist concerns, and the editorial collective affirmed that "Canada does not exist except as a political arrangement for the convenience of individuals accidentally happening to live within its arbitrary area" (Davey 1975:155), a view Bowering reiterated in his 1972 essay "Confessions of a Failed American." Despite the refusal of many of its prominent members to be identified with the nationalist thrust of Canadian culture during its Centennial decade, however, the Vancouver scene was dependent on federal funds, and it reached its peak around 1967 when official support for cultural endeavour was most readily available. Moreover, Vancouver was fortunate in attracting the attention of a Senior Arts Officer of the Canada Council, David Silcox, who not only recognized the city's exceptional potential, but also allowed himself to be infected by its exuberant spirit: a 1966 photograph shows a plastic-wrapped Silcox participating in Iain Baxter's *Bagged Place* (a four-room apartment, complete with bathroom, entirely shrouded in plastic) by pretending to urinate into the toilet (Silcox 1983: 153).

Vancouver's support system was too fragile, however, to sustain the intensity of its scene much beyond the early seventies, by which time characteristic undertakings like Intermedia, the Festival of the Contemporary Arts, and TISH had all ceased to exist and important initiators and artists had moved elsewhere. Their legacy was passed on to subsequent projects

A Community of Correspondences: TISH 15

more strongly oriented towards local concerns and resources than the internationalist sixties had been; some typical post-sixties undertakings included Radio Free Rain Forest, the Western Front gallery, and the Reynoldston Research and Studies' "Oral History of B.C." (Davey 1976:22). By the mid-1970s, it was generally time for reassessment, even nostalgic recollection. Iain and Ingrid Baxter's shortlived Kitsilano restaurant "Eye Scream" may be called a venture in this spirit: echoing sixties' events such as Helen Goodwin's *City Feast* at the Vancouver Art Gallery and the exhibition *Japanese Culinary Pop* at the University of British Columbia, "Eye Scream" served food as conceptual art, and the menu featured Group of Seven Snails, Oysters Michelangelo, Cubist Shrimp Salad and Filet Mignon on Wheels. Also, Talonbooks reprinted the first nineteen issues of TISH in 1975, and the collection *The Writing Life: Historical & Critical Views of the TISH Movement*, published by Black Moss Press, followed a year later. In 1979, Warren Tallman organized a spectacular reunion of the TISH poets and their associates at the Italian Cultural Centre, where, in a series of seven benefit readings for bill bissett, they drew crowds of hundreds and created the mood of a rock concert prolonged over six months. Nor had TISH's opponents abandoned their feud: Keith Richardson's *TISH: Poetry and the Colonized Mind* appeared in 1976. Robin Mathews, the most vocal and influential of Canada's nationalist critics, provided a preface; he also continued to present his objections to TISH's internationalist stance in reviews and articles throughout the seventies and eighties (see, for example, Mathews 1982/83).

All observers agreed that Vancouver's blossoming in the sixties benefitted much from extensive outside contacts. Indeed, Vancouver became more accessible to cross-Canadian and international traffic than it had ever been before: the introduction of DC-8 jets cut flying time between Montreal and Vancouver from ten to six hours, air service between Vancouver and London was provided over the North Pole, and the Trans-Canada Highway from St. John's, Newfoundland, to Victoria, B.C. was completed. The telex anticipated the role which the fax has assumed now, and there was a general enchantment with the new technology which "diversified and enriched man's perceptual world" (Davey 1974: 11). One artist, Iain Baxter, reminisced in 1983: "I put a telex in my house because I felt that you could plug into anywhere in the world and it didn't matter if you were a little tiny town" (Farrell-Ward 137). Baxter also used Telecopier 11 to transmit an image to a New York gallery and to participate in a show without ever travelling there.

Even conventional means of communication such as the mails were redefined by so-called correspondence art, a concept with dadaist roots which sought to undermine, through satire and other subversive means, the hegemony of cultural and political centres. Serious letter-writing campaigns, designed to give the individual citizens access to political decision-making, acquired an air of dadaist iconoclasm: one of the more startling discoveries one can make among Bowering's papers is an exchange with Ferdinand Marcos as "athlete to athlete," because Bowering "also play[ed] baseball as a hobby." Marcos promptly fell into the trap and responded to the poet's admonishments, assuring him that he intended to "rely less on military might and more on uplifting the life of the poor and unfortunate," and thanking him for "giving [him] this chance to take a respite from the burdens of office" (Bowering papers NLC). Moreover, correspondence art challenges individualistic concepts of creativity as one form of power hegemony, and seeks to create "the mechanics of a collective creative consciousness" (*Art and Correspondence* n.p.) by widely disseminating images of various origin through the mails, "usually formalized into original and precise abbreviated vocabulary, utilizing rubber stamps, xerox and other 'rapid data' copying means, maps, circulars, drawings, and notes" ("Concrete Poetry" n.p.). Among noteworthy projects were Glenn Lewis's "The New York Corres Sponge Dance School of Vancouver," Eric and Kate Craig's "Dr. and Lady Brute," and Michael Morris and Vincent Trasov's "Image Bank Correspondence Exchange" but also Glenn Lewis's *Great Wall of 1984*, a mural consisting of 365 plastic boxes filled by various artists and coordinated by Glenn Lewis and, ironically, housed in an eminently centralist institution, the National Research Library in Ottawa.

Correspondence artists even turned travel into a multi-media performance:

> In June [1968] [Michael Morris] spent two weeks in New York where he stayed with Rauschenberg, whom he met originally in L.A.... In New York Morris also went to see Ray Johnson, an artist who had written to him after seeing reproductions of his work in art magazines. Johnson now sends him communications about once a week – anagrams, two or three photos – as part of what he terms his New York Correspondence School. In L.A. Morris visits Kurt von Meier, West Coast correspondent for Art International. (Lowndes 1968: 10)

As visible proof of his belief in art as a communal, non-elitist property, Morris carried "a smashed fragment of a record" in his luggage, a reminder of Ralph Ortiz's *Piano Destruction Concerto,* during which the pianist had demolished both a record player and a piano, the latter a particularly gory affair, because "plastic bags filled with animal blood suspended inside the

A Community of Correspondences: TISH 17

piano burst open under [Ortiz's] efficient strokes" (Lowndes 1983:147). Although critic Joan Lowndes did not refer to Vancouver as a "little tiny town" as Iain Baxter had done (Vancouver's population numbered approximately 900,000 in 1969), she still alluded to its potential isolation when she concluded: "Thus Morris maintains a network of international contacts that enable him, from his apartment in a rambling old house on Locarno Beach, to enjoy the best of Vancouver without becoming provincial" (Lowndes 1968: 10). Outside contacts often provided a catalyst for greater cooperation and exchange within the city, in pubs, jazz-clubs, the VAG noon hour events, or the musician Al Neil and film-maker/poet Sam Perry's Sound Gallery, a place where Bowering enjoyed "weird music ... and wild color projections on the walls" on a return visit from Calgary. The Sound Gallery became one of the origins of Intermedia, an artists' cooperative which promoted and staged multi-media events and strove to provide equal access to expensive technological equipment for all artists.

Not surprisingly, Marshall McLuhan, whose concept of the "global village" implied general accessibility to, and decentralization of, the media, was one of the most influential visitors to the city, as was Buckminster Fuller, and their books *The Gutenberg Galaxy, The Medium is the Massage, Spaceship Earth* and *Intuition* were considered compulsory reading. A venue where McLuhan and Fuller and others like John Cage, Merce Cunningham, Robert Rauschenberg, and Alan Watts presented their views and work was the Festival of the Contemporary Arts at UBC, which was held every February from 1961 until 1972 and which strove to emulate McLuhan's "mosaic or field approach" by bringing together artists from various disciplines to explore a common theme, for "no medium has its meaning or existence alone, but only in constant interplay with other media" (McLuhan 1964: 26). The 1965 Festival of the Contemporary Arts was an homage to McLuhan, featuring "The Medium is the Message," "the first major multi-sensory public happening in Vancouver," (*Vancouver Art* 194), which involved local artists, architects, and choreographers Iain Baxter, Arthur Erickson, Helen Goodwin, and, as designer and coordinator, Abraham Rogatnick. In his recent biography of McLuhan, Philip Marchand provides precious detail about the event:

[Rogatnick and some of his colleagues] took over a cement-floored armory on the university campus and rounded up about thirty slide-projectors. Students operated the projectors from the rafters, from the balcony, from all over the building. As visitors wandered through a maze of huge plastic sheets hanging from the ceiling, they found themselves in the midst of a barrage of random photographic images or abstract designs projected on the floor, the ceiling, the plastic sheets, and, occasionally, themselves. The students wielded these projectors as if they were weapons pressed into service of art. Trucks that drove into the armory for regular deliveries were suddenly transformed into luminous art forms bearing obscure but meaningful messages. (Marchand 1989: 171f)

This event had been prepared by an ambitious programme the previous year, when Rogatnick and McLuhan joined Doris Shadbolt and others in a panel discussion on Pop Art, McLuhan lectured on "Changing Attitudes to Space in Poetry, Painting and Architecture since Television," Gerd Stern of San Francisco recited poetry to the accompaniment of music and visual images, Jean Erdman performed "The Coach with the Six Insides," a comedy of acting, miming and dancing based on Joyce's *Finnegans Wake*, and Pauline Kael lectured on modern film.

Director Alvin Balkind – despite inadequate quarters in the basement of the main library – often coordinated shows at the UBC Fine Arts Gallery to complement the activities at the Festival, and his 1964 showing of Pop Art, "Art becomes Reality," won particular acclaim. Many of his other themes also bear witness to the vital role which his gallery played at the time, and it is worth listing some of them because they mirror the concerns of the poets as well. Bowering was particularly impressed with "The Unquiet Canvas" (1962), an exhibition featuring the work of artists such as Tanabe, Kiyooka, and Bob Steele, who had challenged the rectangular shape and flat surface of the traditional painting much as the TISH group sought to modify the well-wrought poem. "Letter Shapes" (also in 1962) bore the motto that "writing is the painted image of the voice; the more it resembles it, the better it is," echoing a main principle of Olson's "Projective Verse" which was to permeate the Vancouver Poetry Festival the subsequent year. A 1964 showing presented collages and banners by Baxter, bissett, Kiyooka, Onley, Shadbolt, Skelton, and others, the visual equivalents of the historical disruptions which Olson's "Human Universe" postulated as characteristic of the postmodern era. A similar skepticism toward historical development expressed itself in a local response to the Guggenheim Museum's exhibition "Systemic Painting," a show entitled "Systems, Groups, Sequences, Series" (1968), which may be said to complement TISH's interest in the serial poem. Finally, the 1969 display "Concrete Poetry" presented the works of poet-artists bp Nichol, bill bissett, Stephen Scobie, Michael Morris, Ray Johnson, and Yoko Ono, and others.

Beyond Balkind's gallery, contacts between artists and poets were also close. A key figure was Roy Kiyooka who called the 1963 UBC Poetry

A Community of Correspondences: TISH

Conference "a truly momentous occasion for [him]" (Pinney 177) and who invited Robert Creeley, one of its most influential participants, to read at the Vancouver School of Art, where the poet impressed Gary Lee-Nova and others of Kiyooka's colleagues and students. In 1965, Kiyooka contributed collages to one of Bowering's first volumes of poetry, a collaboration which deserves to be discussed separately in a chapter on *The Man in Yellow Boots*.

If the artists sought to participate in an international community, so too did the poets. They were in the vanguard of Vancouver's miraculous decade for, by 1963, the poetry scene centred on TISH had reached a first climax and most of the original editors – Frank Davey, George Bowering, Fred Wah, Lionel Kearns, and Jamie Reid – were leaving town. That year (coincidentally the year of William Carlos Williams' death) UBC staged a poetry conference which became as legendary as the "International Poetry Incarnation," a 1965 reading at the Royal Albert Hall with Ginsberg, Corso and Ferlinghetti. Ginsberg also appeared in Vancouver, as did Robert Duncan, Robert Creeley, Charles Olson, Philip Whalen, Denise Levertov, and Margaret Avison.[2] Most of these had first been presented to a larger public in Donald Allen's anthology *The New American Poetry, 1945-1960* (1960) which, in contrast to Donald Hall, Robert Pack, and Louis Simpson's collection *The New Poets of England and America* issued three years earlier, focused on writers outside the academic tradition and, for Warren Tallman's students, became the initial principal source for both the new poetry and its most significant theories. Some of the speakers at the Vancouver Poetry Festival had been in town before, when the Tallmans used their San Francisco contacts to invite poets willing to conduct workshops at UBC. One such visit, Robert Duncan's in 1961, provided the spark for the foundation of TISH (phonetic inversion of "shit," although Bowering has since facetiously claimed that the abbreviation really stands for "The Truth is Sure Heavy" [Bowering 1985: 15]), a poetry newsletter using the inexpensive production methods and condensed lay-out typical of correspondence art.

The very titles of some of the texts studied by Tallman's students reflected the openness of the era, whether it be Duncan's *The Opening of Field* or "Towards an Open Universe," Olson's "Projective Verse" and *The Distances*, or Kerouac's *On the Road*. In keeping with the communicative spirit of these works, and following the model of other magazines such as Cid Corman's *Origin*, LeRoy Jones and Diane Di Prima's *The Floating Bear*, and Louis Dudek's *Delta*, TISH was conceived of as an "open letter," seeking to establish a network by urging its readers to participate in the making of the magazine. This policy was continued in later publications edited by former members of the TISH group, such as Davey's *Open Letter*, Bowering's *Imago*, or Davey and Wah's *Swift Current*, "an electronic literary magazine accessible by writers and readers with personal computers from nearly any urban area of Canada" (Davey, n.d.: 1).[3] Frank Davey prefaced TISH 1, "TISH will give of itself to its readers FREEly, provided that they will write to its editor at least once every three issues" (Davey 1975: 13), and he was supported by the collective in the second issue: "TISH wants to know what you are doing. Anything – painting, writing, digging, dancing, thinking, – especially if you're MAKING IT" (33). Later, a note from the editors affirmed "TISH is designed primarily as a poetry *newsletter*.... Also we are interested in letters – from poets, critics, philanthropists, anyone; especially letters that include pertinent & particular discussion of work that appears in these pages" (88).

This request for criticism from the outside was an extension of the practise TISH editors pursued in working with each other. Reassessing his affiliation with the magazine in 1978, Bowering concluded: "What TISH mainly offered, to me, was two things: one, being taken seriously by people who[m] I would take seriously ... The other thing was the business of being in a community, being in that community, is a kind of introduction to the commitment to the larger community of the language and of poetry" (Bayard, David 84). In order to underline the collective nature of their undertaking, the editors of TISH occasionally published poems anonymously or under a pseudonym, a practise Bowering continues today, although his reasons may now be different. The formally most interesting result of TISH's cooperative spirit were the "companion poems" or "twin poems," as Robert Duncan called them in his essay "For the Novices of Vancouver, August 25-28, 1962" (Davey 1975: 256). In "Two Poems for the Critic," "Two Poems for a Bicycle Rider," "Two Dialectics for Bridges," and "Two Poems for a City," Bowering and Frank Davey responded to the same subject as well as responding to each other's vision of it: Bowering's contribution to the "Two Dialectics for Bridges" drew a satirical anti-poem from Davey in "A Repudiation for G.B." in the next issue. The title of Duncan's essay alludes to Novalis's "Die Jünglinge zu Sais," and Bowering too linked the procedure to the Romantics, namely the complementary relationship of Wordsworth's "Ode on Intimations of Immortality" and Coleridge's "Dejection: an Ode" (Bayard, David 84). The parallel between TISH and the Romantics has been suggestively explored in Quartermain's "Romantic Offensive: TISH" (Quartermain 1977), and it would be daunting to go a step further and to view the work of the TISH poets as part of the same

A Community of Correspondences: TISH

canon, much in the way in which Paul Magnuson, in *Coleridge and Wordsworth: A Lyrical Dialogue* (1988), has explored the dialogic interdependence of the two English romantics from a Bakhtinian perspective.

A more extensive and closely knit web of responses was established when poets allowed their individual concerns (such as Davey's bridge poems, Wah and Dawson's dance lyrics, Lane's *études* on margins) to interact with those of their companions. The most catalytic text in this respect was Davey's essay "The Problem of Margins," which elicited another from Fred Wah entitled "Margins into Lines: A Relationship" as well as poems by Bowering and by Lane; one of the key phrases in *Points on the Grid* (1964), a collection of Bowering's poems for TISH and of other lyrics, is "the margins of my mind" (see "What is he …," "Telephone Metaphysic," "Wood," "Metathesis," "Walking Poem"). The "margins of the mind" define the poet's limitations "which hem him inside the boundary," but also challenge him "to cut / to make a way / a path / a surging across" ("Points on the Grid"). In its discussion of "margins," TISH responded in part to Duncan's *The Opening of the Field* (1960): the cover of that book combined a circle of dancing children with an abstract design of foliage drawn toward a magnetic centre, emblems of "a field of energy, of activity, of the imagination" (Gunn 1299). For Bowering, Duncan's image became a perfect reflection of his poetic creed. All of Vancouver served as a field of energy, much as Paterson had played that role for Williams and Gloucester for Olson. Ocean and bridges particularly reflected the city's function as "an actual place that is also a spiritual beachhead" (Duncan 253). In "L.S." (= "Locus Solus"), the poet participates in the cycle of ocean and rain bounding the city, his figure underneath a dripping umbrella tracing the outline of a magic ellipse: "under billowed concave black / umbrella dripping around me." His eyes are fixed "down on neon reflections / wiggled in the gutter," and from the reflection rises the memory of "dried out lips & tongue / long trip without water- / bottle down the side of old Blue Mountain." The field of energy radiates downward into the earth, strengthening the poet's vertical stance, but it also horizontally extends beyond his immediate context, an axis Bowering explored in an essay entitled "Universal and Particular: An Enquiry into a Personal Esthetic" (Bowering 1965b), excerpts of which were published in TISH. The idea of an intersecting axis of the "universal" and the "particular" gave rise to one of Bowering's favourite images, that of the poet as tree,

A tree
an oak tree

an oak with a tree house
nailed between its branches
                      stands
                      in the field
                      of my mind,
                      growing, or
                      staying grown
    ("Metaphor 1," TISH 5)

Here, the compact section outlining the crown of the tree is followed by a "trunk" placed too far to the right to serve as a naturalistic imitation of a tree trunk, "because a poem is not an imitation of anything; it is an interaction, it is the *personal* song of a man interacting with the universe around and inside him" (Davey 1975: 103). Bowering's lyric then is a living thing, "the very riding thru me of the / meta-phor / thru me & away on a trip / past the margins of the mind."

Etymologically, a "metaphor" is a "change of place," and with their insistence on means of communication such as telephones ("Telephone Metaphysic"), cars ("Driving Past"), bicycles ("Motor Age"), bridges and streets ("Tuesday Night"), and the radio ("Radio Jazz"), Bowering's TISH poems spin a web of connections across the city, although they are usually deferred, tenuous, or imagined, blockages signalling boundary or margin.

But standing in a gaslit phonebooth
I still ask you to tell me how you are wearing your hair
        You are not really there
        but I push against the margins of my mind
    ("Telephone Metaphysic")

"Telephone Metaphysic" translates the axis of the universal and particular into a juxtaposition of the square shape of a phone booth and the distant allure of the young woman's voice. The most programmatic and masterly rendition of the idea, however, occurs in a poem not specifically alluding to the city of Vancouver, but still making full use of the images Bowering developed to describe it. "Points on the Grid" counterpoints the rigidity of a grid-system (a pin-board) with dynamic movement and organic growth. Although the poem pertly – and with a staccato of alliteration and monosyllabics – speaks of the product of the creative moment as if it were a dead butterfly, "a place to put the finger / and pin the poem," "Points on the Grid" is printed "in ... a wavering line." The pattern imitates the "waves" and "breakers" which push against the stasis of the grid, and Ulysses'

A Community of Correspondences: TISH 23

exploratory ride across the Aegean is contrasted with the crucifixion of Vitruvian man in a graph ironically designed to prove his superiority to all of nature. Yet the poem reprises the phrase "to pin the poem" (or variations thereof) three times, and Ulysses' quest, "unmindful of that sought for point / at the end," is still headed for Ithaca where Penelope knits rows "inexorable as the waves / her needles making points in the graph." Many of the verbs are either infinitives or participles of the present, but they too partake of the dialectic informing this poem, for while the grammatical form may suggest indetermination or intensely prolonged moments, the meaning of the word does not. Thus "to cut / to make a way" stand beside "to put the finger / and pin," and "surging," "bounding," "wavering" and "unraveling" stand beside "pinning."

"Points on the Grid" may be called a particularly complex product of the cooperative "field" provided by the TISH collective, but their interdependence did not always meet with approval by the outside critics whom the editors so eagerly urged to speak their minds. When Davey's piece, "The Problem of Margins", launched the discussion on margins, a disgruntled reader complained "Why is it you all feed on each others' derivative little drippings? Don't you have minds of your own? Can't you function independently at least of each other?" (Davey 1975: 93). A similar criticism came from David Bromige, when Bowering and Red Lane exchanged "open letters" to each other in a series of poems. These two readers clearly failed to understand TISH's communal philosophy, and instead posited the poet as individualist creator, a concept, like that of the poetic community, ironically also rooted in Romanticism and reconfirmed in modernism. Yet TISH's critics did draw attention to a significant qualification in the statement "TISH will give of itself to its readers FREEly," for the invitation was "open" only to a specific audience. Like correspondence artists, the TISH collective constructed their own readership by compiling a list of desired subscribers, mailing them the issues free-of-charge, and requesting donations to keep the operation afloat. And as Bowering explained in a 1976 interview with Barry McKinnon, the fourteen pages of a typical TISH issue were constructed to give prominence to writers who were congenial, but little or no attention to those who were not: "We print poems which conform to our taste, poems which move somewhat in the same direction as our own" (Davey 1975: 91). Like other little magazines, TISH was created as an alternative to the academic journals and the mainstream literary activity, but in order to do so, it had to practise "auto-marginalization" (Lista 8) and mimic the exclusivity of the very publications it challenged. This paradox explains why TISH, despite its "democratic" concept, has on occasion been charged with elitism,[4] a reproach which has followed its editors well into their present career. One such attack came from Al Purdy, who countered Bowering's prescriptive review of Milton Acorn's *Against a League of Liars* ("[Poets] should know that some statements will fit better into a sociological dissertation than into free verse, and vice versa" [Davey 1975: 76]), with a broadside in TISH 5: "May we then expect in due and scholarly course a lengthy treatise delineating the exact limits beyond which poetry may not transgress? This would serve as a guide and mentor for the young, a warning sentinel for those as old as Acorn" (92). The exchange spawned a correspondence between Bowering and Purdy which may well be one of the most important extended discussions of, and feuds in, Canadian poetics (Bowering papers NLC). Amusingly, Bowering did provide "in due and scholarly course" a book such as the one Purdy had sarcastically requested: it was a study of Purdy (1970a), whom Bowering took to task for violating the laws of projective verse.

Bowering's correspondence with Al Purdy forms a significant part of the enormous correspondence Bowering was to keep with congenial authors (Bowering papers NLC), and in a sense, his personal letters are an extension of the various "open letters" he has edited throughout his career. His correspondence is clearly also part of his *oeuvre*, or better yet, in competition with it. "I've decided to keep writing," he informed *El Corno Emplumado* in 1967, "but no longer ... to keep restrictions of forming, making, crafting, good poems. I'm just going to write writing ... Maybe I'll just be writing letters" (Bowering 1967c: 141). Especially in the exchanges with Red Lane, Margaret Randall, David McFadden, and Al Purdy, the letters are cross-generic and, like Pound's, "constitute [part of] a poetic mode continuous from Canto to manifesto to letter to critical essay, a mode that provides us with a paradigm of what *writing* can be ... in a time when established boundaries are undergoing erasure" (Perloff 1985b: 86). It is probably no coincidence that two recent studies of cultural intertextuality, Jacques Derrida's *La Carte postale: De Socrate à Freud et au-delà* (1980) and Madeleine Ouellette-Michalska's *L'Amour de la carte postale* (1987), focus on a popular means of correspondence as a central image.

Like Kiyooka and McFadden (authors of *transcanadaletters* and *Letters from the Earth to the Earth* respectively), Bowering assigns a metaphysical quality to letters which are "correspondences" in the sense of spiritual analogy as well as earthly communication. In a chaotic universe, they function as signals of synchronicity, hence fragile cohesion, and Bowering underlines both these qualities by enclosing *objets trouvés* (bus tickets,

A Community of Correspondences: TISH 25

photographs, advertisements) in his own letters. Because Bowering's letters often address the same subject with different correspondents, they echo his "companion poems" with Davey. At the same time, they resemble William Carlos Williams' 1938-1947 exchange with David Lyle, a communications specialist who "addressed simultaneously persons often unknown to each other and in widely divergent fields." Lyle's work consisted in correlating the responses and discovering common elements in even the most disparate statements. Williams', and Bowering's, interest in extensive letter-writing, especially the resulting "correlations of trivia with permanence" (Weaver 123), is linked to their focus on the news, a topic which will be of major significance in the chapter on *Rocky Mountain Foot*.

In the decade before TISH, vanguard American poets – many of whom were going to be mentors to the TISH poets – also maintained contact through the mails. The most voluminous and important exchange was probably that of Olson and Duncan, and both Olson's *The Maximus Poems* and Duncan's *Derivations: Selected Poems 1950-56* include, or allude to, letters and postcards. The cosmic vocabulary they used in describing their network anticipates that of Kiyooka, McFadden, and Bowering (who receives a letter from Robert Duncan in his poem "Apollo 11"). Thus, Denise Levertov wrote of her correspondence with Duncan that it was "a constellation rather than ... a linear sequence. And in that constellation the major stars are without question the messages of instruction by means of which my intelligence grew keener, my artistic conscience more acute; messages of love, support, and solidarity in the fellowship of poetry" (quoted in Harris 196). These "messages of love, support, and solidarity" did not, however, exclude sharp mutual criticism, nor the establishment of master-student hierarchies. The early letters in Olson's *The Maximus Poems* assume the authoritative voice of the biblical epistle "decrying the wickedness, warning of retribution, offering moral guidance" (Miller 1979: 215). A similar tone appears in Red Lane's poems and letters to Bowering (collected in part, in *Letters from Geeksville: Red Lane to George Bowering, 1960-64* [1976]) whose echo resonates throughout the remainder of Bowering's oeuvre, well into *Kerrisdale Elegies*.

The first issue of TISH contained "Radio Jazz"[5] a poem which was to remain one of Bowering's best and which alluded to yet another area in which he and his contemporaries explored "a community of correspondences." In *Paterson*, Williams included an extract from Mezz Mezzrow's *Really the Blues;* Kerouac admired Charlie Parker and Lester Young and declared the jazz pianist George Shearing a god; together with Patchen and Rexroth, Kerouac recorded poetry and jazz sessions. Ginsberg's *Howl*, besides drawing on the visionary poetry of Smart, Blake, Shelley, and Whitman, imitated the repeated cadences in Lester Young's saxophone improvisations (Portugés 86). In jazz, the poets found inspiration for their notions of "spontaneous prose," "projective verse," and the "variable foot": "The voice saxophone," Warren Tallman wrote in TISH, "reacting on down to the solar plexus and on up to the lips, will project the writers's inner resonance if he is sensitive enough to the almost limitless sound possibilities in the range of notes and tones that opens out from close consideration of, say, the phonetic alphabet" (Tallman 1961: 67). As contributors to TISH emphasized over and over in their poems and in their critical statements, the new poetry was oral, and it shared with jazz its improvisational and dialogic qualities as well as the knowledge that it was art for outsiders,[6] for bebop, the music of Dizzy Gillespie, Thelonious Monk, and Charlie Parker, was emphatically opposed to commercial swing. Bowering experimented with jazz rhythms in *Mirror on the Floor* (1967), repeatedly paying homage to the music of Miles Davis, Sonny Rollins, and Jimmy Giuffre, but his most impressive adaptation of jazz occurs in *How I Hear "Howl"* (1969). In writing about Ginsberg's poem, Bowering used the recording of the 1968 Chicago reading; belligerently separating himself from academic criticism, he responded to, rather than analysed, the performance as if his voice were one blues instrument engaged in dialogue with another:

But woe betide the scholar man who says a man dont have time to see precise truth when he is lipping off this way. Let me say the great poet (& in this poem speaks he) comes to truth world thru the sounds he picks out of it. So I will mention some things I hear in.... *Howl*, & I say that in his rapid setting down, Ginsberg was in the happy poet experience where the true sounds of the galaxy are there with true sightings, & the man's pen is hard presst to get most he can down, in frantic pursuit. (Bowering 1969a: 222-23)

CHAPTER TWO

Cubist Collage: *The Man in Yellow Boots*

We were sitting in the warm house of *El Corno Emplumado*, Mexico City, with editors Sergio Mondragón and Meg Randall (in real life, Señora Mondragón). The cover [for *Imago* 2] was to be printed in Mexico, and we decided it would have a Mexican figure in the lower right hand corner. I said that what I wanted was a picture of a butterfly, because a butterfly was the perfect representation of an imago, that product of metamorphosis. We decided to look thru the drawings in a beautiful book called *El Universo de Quetzalcoatl* ... [and found] a drawing taken from a stone carving at Monte Alban in Oaxaca. He represents the final metamorphosis, sex, soul, art, life and death. In the drawing the butterfly, symbol of fire, has replaced the male genitals. We were all surprised. Sergio said it was a manifestation, and Sergio is Mexican; he has old blood in him. (*Imago* 2)

Among Bowering's first volumes of poetry, *The Man in Yellow Boots* (1965a) is the most successfully designed, both in the choice of its poems and in its appearance. Although published when Bowering was already teaching in Calgary, it is a perfect expression of the communal spirit of the Vancouver years, as well as a compact encyclopedia of the poetic concerns dominating later volumes that were now beginning to appear in rapid succession. Chief among these concerns are the short erotic lyric, which was to be at the centre of *The Silver Wire* (1966); political satire, the focus of *Rocky Mountain Foot* (1968), and, perhaps most importantly, the elegy, examples of which were to appear in practically all of Bowering's collections from now on. A major impetus for the latter were the deaths of Bowering's father and of Red Lane, and *The Man in Yellow Boots* is dedicated to Lane's memory. However, the book is also an elegy for, and homage to, W. C. Williams, whose presence is felt in almost every poem in the volume, but particularly in "For WCW" and "The Descent." If "Circus Maximus" in TISH 17 described the passing of poetic legacy as the playful interaction of acrobats, this volume defines it as a passage "to wisdom as to despair" ("The Descent").

The Man in Yellow Boots / El hombre de las botas amarillas appeared as a special issue of the Mexican poetry magazine *El Corno Emplumado* edited by Margaret Randall and Sergio Mondragón, whom Bowering initially contacted through the inter-American network of avantgardist poetry magazines. In keeping with the dual principle embodied in the name of the publication, a combination of "the horn, the instrument of American jazz, & the plumes of Quetzacoatl, symbol of Mexican culture, or better, precolumbian Latin American culture" (Castro 6), Mondragón provided translations into Spanish of the poems and of letters Bowering had written to *El Corno* while the issue was being assembled. The latter chronicle his current concerns as a teacher, writer and sportsfan, but they especially show him in conflict with the reactionary mentality he perceived in his Albertan environment. This was a facet of his activities which Randall and Mondragón, both fervent Marxists, were particularly interested in underlining, and their preface noted approvingly:

The poems in Bowering's first book, *Points on the Grid* ... were written out of the time when the poet's concern was largely involved with the technique of poetry, handling the language, finding his own place in it.... The poems in this new book deal with more meaningful concerns, not the problem of how to write poetry, but involved with direct emotions; politics, love, etc. (Bowering 1965a: n.p.).

Understandably, Randall and Mondragón stressed those aspects in Bowering's work closest to their own preferences; nevertheless, *The Man in Yellow Boots* has a metapoetic dimension, sometimes particularly strongly present in poems "involved with direct emotions." This combination of the concrete and reflexive appears even in the title and cover design of the book. *The Man in Yellow Boots* alludes to an earlier period in Bowering's life when he also refused to concur with regimentation: as a member of the Royal Canadian Air Force, he sprayed his regulation snow boots yellow, a deadly colour for a military man and one of the many paradoxes characteristic of this collection. Suitably, Bowering's letters to *El Corno* are printed on yellow paper; the word "yellow" in the title appears in that colour as well, and it acquires additional resonance from the fact that elsewhere in Bowering's *oeuvre*, in "Vancouver Étude" (*The Silver Wire*) and "On a Black Painting by Tamayo" (*Points on the Grid*), yellow functions as the equivalent of a void or gap to be filled in by the perceiver: "a game to wake and play / the yellow thing." Precisely because of its ambiguous connotations, yellow is Bowering's favourite colour. At Sir George Williams, he painted three walls of his window-less office in a particularly bright hue of yellow, complemented by a blue fourth wall. A yellow-and-blue shirt

Cubist Collage: *The Man in Yellow Boots*   29

allowed him to become virtually invisible in this startling setting. Viewer participation is also required by the remainder of the words printed on the cover of *The Man in Yellow Boots:* defying the straight Gutenberg line, they dance across the page, forming wavering or half-circular patterns ineffectually held in check by hand-drawn underscorings.

Sylvia de Swaan, a Roumanian photographer and painter living in Mexico, photographed a pair of boots for the cover, showing them straight-on and crossed with the nonchalance of a casual *flâneur* on the front cover, and squarely planted apart on the back, but here seen from above, as a man might look down at his own feet. These postures convey stasis, if in varying degrees, but there is also a strong suggestion of momentum. Both pictures are fragments, and the perceiver's glance travels beyond the margins of the page, which is foregrounded as an arbitrary excerpt of a larger image. Because the two pictures correspond to different perspectives, the cover design of *The Man in Yellow Boots* invites the reader to encircle and explore the book as if it were a cubist sculpture. This is a quality worth dwelling on in some detail, not only because *The Man in Yellow Boots* is now a rarity, but also because later volumes adopted a similar approach. For *The Gangs of Kosmos,* for instance, Charles Pachter provided a lithograph entitled *Champêtre,* on the front cover of which a woman (Margaret Atwood) looks directly at the observer, while on the back another (Angela Bowering) looks away from him. If the cover is spread out to reveal the complete lithograph, a tiny Charles Pachter appears, crucified on the spine and linking the glances of both women.

Just as the cover design of *The Man in Yellow Boots* challenges conventions of space, so too, in their own way, do the poems. The first poem, "To Cleave," and the last, "Breaking Up, Breaking Out," formulate, as it were, the programme of the volume. In each, Bowering puns on a central word, revealing it to be an oxymoronic combination of fusion and separation, destruction and growth: according to *Webster's* "to cleave" means "to divide by ... a cutting blow," as well as "to adhere firmly and closely or loyally and unwaveringly" while "Breaking Up, Breaking Out" is

Breaking Up
of nations, sickness, log jam,
my psyche

the way of the world
order,
form

But "Breaking Up, Breaking Out" is also the growth of a tree "layer on layer, ring reaching / farther than previous ring." Both poems develop a central analogy between the organic and the spiritual; they are metaphysical lyrics and Bowering's observations about Margaret Avison's poetry apply to his own as well: "the poet wants to welcome and hopes to produce epiphanies, less-than-moments when there is light from eternity shining through a rent in the fabric of time" (Bowering 1972c: 9). Mystic and cosmic vocabulary appears in several of Bowering's poems to describe the poet's humility, even self-effacement, before creation. There is the ascetic scenario of "Poor Man," and the paradoxic reversal in "Moon Shadow," where the proud assertion "I am able to instruct / the whole universe" – reinforced by a series of parallel constructions ("I am moon!", "I slide cold & pale," "I show one face," "I am shining tear") – is followed by

my shadow before me

on the earth, moon shadow
rainbow round my heart,
wondering where in the universe I am.

Here, the supremacy of the "I" has been so effaced that it is not even clear who or what the participle of the present "wondering" refers to. This, then, is a universe not linked by the mind-control of rhyme, but by "rime," accidental correspondence "clutcht out of chaos" ("For WCW"). A central technique of rime is the pun, unexpectedly and briefly fusing the particular with the universal in such homonyms as "tear": "I am a shining tear / of the sun" and "I am able to instruct / ... / the weeping eye / of any single man" ("Moon Shadow"). Less dramatic but similar in effect are repetitions of words, sounds, and rhythms within (linguistically often minimally) altered contexts, such as the word "round," the letters "k," "n" and "h," and the clusters of three subsequent stresses applied to *both* the perceiver and the moon in the first three stanzas of "Moon Shadow":

Last night the rainbow
round the moon

climbed with how sad steps
as I walkt home

color surrounding me
cloud around my head

Like nature's things, the laws of the perceiving mind can never be fully known: it is as ambivalent as the moon: "female / male animal ball / of rock." As in his TISH poems "The Sunday Poem" and "Metaphor 1," Bowering often focuses on a tree or flower to describe the poet's participation in his environment. It is particularly appropriate that the last poem in *The Man in Yellow Boots* should be "Breaking Up, Breaking Out," a lyric which compares the expanding body of a tree to the evolution of self and, in so doing, denies closure of nature, mind, poem and book. In the most striking of his flower poems, "Inside the Tulip," Bowering creates a gigantic blossom reminiscent of Georgia O'Keeffe's flower paintings and of W. C. Williams' flower poems, "The Crimson Cyclamen," "The Petunia," "The Love Song," "Asphodel, That Greeny Flower," and many others. Flowers in Williams have been – somewhat pretentiously – described as "suffused-encircling shapes of mind":

Exploring an intimacy between phenomena and his own consciousness, the poet inhabits a space which is distinct from both his own previous experience and the object contemplated. This two-fold space of the object and the poet's perception is encircled by and suffused with consciousness. (Nelson 552)

In "Inside the Tulip," the perceiver has indeed blended with the perceived, and the fluted interior of the flower has been transformed into the hollow of the lover's mouth: "Let me ... Kiss you / press my tongue on pollen / against the roof of my mouth." Bowering further translates this union into repetition with a difference, shifting from "Let me share this flower / with you" to "Let me share you / with this flower." The setting is Edenic, but, as in "The Descent," Bowering reinterprets Christian dogma. There, his father is reborn, "but not as his mother told us;" in "Inside the Tulip," Adam and Eve are made "part of [the garden's] moving beauty" (Bowering 1985: 79), not its owners and managers.

Closely linked to the flower metaphor is that of the dance. One of the most influential choreographers of the sixties, Merce Cunningham, liked "to turn his dancers into flowers unfolding on their stalks" (Buckle n.p.), and the names of several of his works during the decade reflect his concern with natural movements and settings: *Field Dances* (1963), *Winterbranch* (1964), *Rain Forest* (1968). Probably inspired by *Desert Music* (1954), a volume which continued Williams's life-long interest in modern dance (well documented from such early publications as *Sour Grapes* [1921] onwards) the dance metaphor was central to TISH, particularly to Dave Dawson and Fred Wah's work. Bowering too contributed an exploration of the image in "the dance complete," a poem later reprinted in *The Silver Wire* (1966), where feminity, erotic attraction and love-making are frequently likened to dance; at the same time, Eros and dance appear as analogies of the perfect poem, in which a natural order moves according to its own rhythm:

Dance, lady, Dance, you are poem maker
sculpting among furniture, air.
>	my body of fulcrums
>	& weight
>
>>	ready to assist
>>	dance with you
>>	slide thigh on thigh,
>>	up & down
>>	to the floor
>>	end
>>	of dance.

("when you run naked," *The Silver Wire*)

One of Bowering's most important essays of the time, "Dance to a Measure" (1964b), which uses a quotation from *Paterson* in the title and refers to Williams' poem throughout, draws a parallel between Williams' "variable foot," Olson's "projective verse," and the inherent laws of the universe: "The dance of life and relative universe do not deny order; they simply insist on an order of their own begun before men began expressing themselves" (Bowering 1964b: 13). In his turn, Cunningham encouraged his dancers to use spontaneous gestures and movement and asked them to return to pre-balletic forms, much as the Black Mountain Poets, whose work he had encountered during summer appointments at the college, suggested that their disciples explore alternatives to the conventional metric foot. The union between dance and poetry became especially apparent at some of the electrifying "happenings" of the era: at the Royal Albert Hall reading, a young woman responded to Allen Ginsberg's recitation by "moving slowly in a weird twisting dance" (Cook 158) and Warren Tallman describes a poetry reading with Jackson MacLow at UBC, in which the participants, inspired by John Cage's music "[strolled] the aisle, read individually on impulse" (Tallman 1972: 89).

In *The Man in Yellow Boots,* the dance metaphor does not appear as overtly as in *The Silver Wire,* but it is still implied in the erotic poems and occasionally translated into an encircling motion, as in "David" ("'I wonder,' she says / 'can you walk / all around it?'") or into the swaying motion of a swing, as in the poem inspired by Renoir's "La Balançoire," in which dance and flower metaphors are particularly closely linked. Here, a young girl poised on a swing "leans coyly / or thoughtfully away," and a child glances beyond the picture frame, "her eyes the only ones / looking outward." In "Dance to a Measure," Bowering describes French Impressionist paintings as suggesting "first drafts" and "unfinished" work (10). In this poem, too, meanings and conclusions are suspended as is the motion of a swing [1]; in this, "The Swing" resembles Ginsberg's "Cézanne's Ports," in which the meeting place of shore with shore "isn't represented; / it doesn't occur on the canvas" (Ginsberg 1961: 12). Almost every observation about Renoir's painting in "The Swing" is qualified: "seem to stand," "could be fifteen," "coyly or thoughtfully," "some kind of wonder." A key word is "or," which helps to enumerate possibilities without subjugating any alternative to another. In the earlier "On a Black Painting by Tamayo," (*Points on the Grid*), Bowering describes an "unquiet canvas," reminding him

> ... of a game waiting to be played again
>   or is it passive or is it only
>   a game to wake and play
>   the yellow thing
> or I think it is a game to wait to wake
>   to play

In their search for the closest approximation, Bowering's poems "always [try] for the not quite possible exact correspondence" (Bowering 1964b: 147). This may be why he occasionally insists on the ostentatious syntactic markers of the simile and even adopts the language of biblical parable to pair off the two links of an analogy:

>   as the body of a tree
>
> grows outward
> layer on layer, ring reaching
> farther than previous ring –
>
> This is the way
> we break too
>   ("Breaking Up, Breaking Out").

Grammatically speaking, "as the body of the tree," followed by "This is the way," is a violation of parallelism: the analogy, introduced by the magisterial cadence of "as the body of a tree," is marred, hence indicative of "the not quite possible exact correspondence," for "there are always certainties in nature's things (even himself!) that [the perceiver] can never know" (Bowering 1964b: 143). A similar strategy is indicated by Bowering's erratic use of the enjambment, particularly striking in the erotic poems where the restlessness conveyed by the abrupt line endings is in deliberate conflict with the contentment suggested by the scene described, thus producing the "traction/fitting itself against resistance" Bowering praised in Williams's poetry:

I see she is
different in the
morning. Her head
of yellow hair
on the pillow
   ("What is it")

While the poems exploring the three-dimensionality of flower, dance and sculpture explore "order [as] process" (Bowering 1964b: 141), others foreground atrophied formal concepts, in which the dance of life is denied. The circular motion described in "David" for instance counter-balances the sculpture's reproduction in a book, where

He lies flat
on page fifty,

crammed in there
like the written word.

Or, in "Indian Summer," we read:

The Indians I think
are dead, you cant
immortalize them, a
leaf presst between
pages becomes a
page.

Atrophy means death, and the playful serenity of the love lyrics in *The Man in Yellow Boots* is off-set by the almost gothic terror of some of the elegiac poems included in this volume, in which the poet not only laments the deaths of his friend and father, but also his own inexorable decay:

There's not much time
not much time ...

... fingers pasting my picture
in the photo album of death!
   ("Old Time Photo of the Present")

"The Shifting Air" imitates in its long narrow shape "a grotto corridor," from which individual lines try to escape as does the poet from his nightmare, and in "The Kitchen Table," the wandering lines echo his search for his own self in an apparently familiar environment which has suddenly become labyrinthine. In poems such as these, the poet's glance is relentlessly forced into one direction, backwards or inwards, and the dance of life is suspended.

Both the love lyrics and the elegiac poems are intensely personal and, repeating the elliptic shapes evoked in some of the TISH poems, sometimes seem suspended on the white page as if encircled by a protective shell: "That is form / the shape of the thing / finished. An eggshell / in the hand, warm /" ("the dance complete," TISH 19). Other pieces, however, juxtapose such privacy with public events, often of extreme violence. Among these are "Her Act was a Bomb," "The Good Prospects," "The Day Before the Chinese A-Bomb," and "Vox Crapulous (alternate title: J. Edgar Hoover)." The presence of these political and aggressive poems affects one's reading of the love lyrics and elegies as well, for the former now appear even more precious, but also more fragile, and the elegies become part of a general lament for the times. In "Her Act was a Bomb," Bowering abruptly juxtaposes three unrelated but synchronous occurrences, ranging from the banal to the catastrophic. These three events are loosely linked with the coordinates "and" and "but," and no effort is made to create a logical connection, although the enjambments between stanzas two and three and between stanza three and the final line do suggest an inexorable *enchaînement*. The poem imitates filmic montage, in which the mundane and the momentous mutually devalue and elevate each other.

All over America I know
people are switching off the sound
when Sophie Tucker appears
on the Ed Sullivan reruns.

It is of course
an honest gesture, severe
perhaps. But in Las Vegas
I saw an old heron woman

pull down the lever
on a cafe slot machine
and fifteen miles away
on the desert, America

dropt a Bomb on Nevada.

The twin of montage is collage, and for *The Man in Yellow Boots*, the author obtained the collaboration of Roy Kiyooka, who contributed twelve collages, in which the juxtaposition of personal and public is further explored. Kiyooka requested, however, that the images not be used as illustrations to the poems: "It is my feeling that they should be included in the book in one solid block and not be scattered throughout the book. Like they could serve as a breather midway through the poems" (Bowering papers NLC). Inserted between the poem "Old Cracker Barrel" (a satirical combination of love lyric and political poem relatively rare in Bowering's *oeuvre*) and its Spanish translation, the collages provide more than a "breather": they interrupt the sequence established by the poems, shift the discussion onto another plane and, while demanding an attention all of their own, also sharpen the reader's perception for certain visual and structural qualities of Bowering's work which may have escaped him so far. However, the collages also establish alternatives to the poems, creating tensions which inform Kiyooka's own word/image compositions in "Letters purporting to be abt Tom Thomson" (1972) and *The Fontainebleau Dream Machine* (1977), where collage and text often challenge or subvert each other.[2]

In making his request that his images remain autonomous, Kiyooka respected the overall design of *The Man in Yellow Boots* as collage. Like Cage, Rauschenberg, and Cunningham who considered their individual contributions "Separate entities ... not [to] be assembled until the first performance," Bowering and Kiyooka collaborated "in isolation from one another" (Kisselgoff 1), leaving the final effect of their undertaking to chance. It seems fitting that their careers have coincidentally moved in tandem, and it is equally fitting that they have not been completely synchronous: after "apprenticeship" years at the Istituto Allende in Mexico and the Emma Lake Workshops in Saskatchewan, Kiyooka became instructor at the Vancouver School of Art, at Sir George Williams University in Montreal, and the Nova Scotia College of Art and Design, before returning to Vancouver to take up a position in the Fine Arts Department of the University of British Columbia. In collaborating with Bowering on *The Man in Yellow Boots*, Kiyooka exercised an intellectual and spiritual discipline which has been symptomatic of his entire work and teaching and has made him a mentor, even guru, to his younger contemporaries. About his years at the Vancouver School of Art, where Claude Breeze, Brian Fisher, and Bodo Pfeiffer were among his pupils, he said: "the so-called West Coast Landscape School had lost its hold on a new generation who were looking for a relevant aesthetic and ... i, unwittingly, became their collaborator. I brought the hype of the contemporary with me and shoved it under the trees with everything else" (*Kiyooka* n.p.).

Each one of the collages is enclosed in the oval frame preferred by many

Cubist Collage: *The Man in Yellow Boots* 37

of the original collagistes who used it to off-set the often severely geometrical planes contained in it and to underline "the new weightlessness of Cubist forms, whose clustering toward the center of pictorial space tended to contradict the traditional function of the bottom of the picture as a support for the pictorial weight above" (Rosenblum 89). Kiyooka's images incorporate monotype improvisation, a technique which normally furthers the impression of such "weightlessness": "I poured commercial enamel onto a sheet of glass, moved it about with brushes and spatula, then presst paper onto it" (*Kiyooka* n.p.). But the monotypes are combined with magazine cuttings, the violence or ambiguity of which undermine the free play of the improvisations: the amorphous scrawls and blotches in most of the collages assume the shapes of flames, blood stains, or finger prints; occasionally the oval resembles a lens enlarging a diseased cell underneath. The focus and perspective in the magazine cuttings change with the dizzying frequency of a television image; some of the news photographs dissolve into dotted print, and overall the collages belie their stasis on the page with a pulsating presence deeply disquieting to the observer. Like Bowering's complex play with the word "tear" in "Moon Shadow," so too the collages may be said to suggest both an eye mournfully reflecting impending catastrophe and an angry rent in the dense verbal and visual fabric of propaganda: two collages show a crowd waiting or listening, spellbound; in another, a parachutist hurtles toward a target; and enormous letters serve as a fence or cage for the crumpled débris behind them in one of the last images. As the 1961 exhibition *The Art of Assemblage* at New York's Museum of Modern Art indicated, topical allusions and political satire were as essential to the neo-Dadaists as they had been to their forebears:

> often [the collages] are fearfully dark, evoking horror or nausea: the anguish of the scrap heap; the images of charred bodies that keep Hiroshima and Nagasaki before our eyes ... symbols of democracy, national power, and authority [are represented] with mild amusement or irony, with unconcealed resentment and scatological bitterness, or simply as totally banal pictures. (Seitz 89)

The first image contains particularly complex political commentary. Divided by a horizontal bar, it combines a photograph of a nuclear explosion in the upper half with the picture of a human torso in the lower. The torso seems to be propped up against a vertical, trunk-like bar, so that the explosion evokes the crown of a tree, a coincidental and sharply ironical commentary on Bowering's comparatively pastoral use of the image. The torso resembles the Belvedere torso, one of the most celebrated cultural icons of western civilization. Here, however, its forceful energy dissolves into a strange shroud wrapped around its loins, an effect not dissimilar to the wrapping and shrouding with which Dadaists, Man Ray foremost among them, destroyed the aura of canonical art. In Kiyooka's collage, the torso assumes a double function, for far from asserting the supremacy of man as the Belvedere torso has traditionally been called upon to do, it seems both origin and victim of the explosion. Instead of its powerful trunk, the torso's missing limbs are foregrounded; it loses its value as icon of tradition retrieved (Rosand) and becomes a mutilated, suffering body instead. The first collage acquires additional power from another torso, or rather several of them, in an image of such violence that it threatens to bleed onto the plain white surrounding them: "One of [the collages] one of the most horrific uses a photo of Malcolm X dead and beside it to the left a shadowy photo of a guy shooting heroin in his arm. This in the upper half of the lunet. In the lower half, separated by a narrow strip is the sleeve of a well-tailored shirt set horizontally with its telling well-creased wrinkles" (Kiyooka to Bowering, Bowering papers NLC). (The image stayed so strongly with Bowering that it resurfaces in his poem "Martin Luther King" in *The Gangs of Kosmos*). The fragmented bodies in Kiyooka's collages have yet another effect, for they also place the design of the whole book into a new light. The boots on the cover, so far read as a playful, even weightless image, suddenly become menacing. The creases in the leather establish a visual link to the creases in the "well-tailored shirt;" in both cases, the wearer remains anonymous. Particularly disquieting seems the image on the back cover now, for the reader is forced into the shoes of a person he does not know.

The collages for *The Man in Yellow Boots* were produced at a time when the oval was an important *leitmotif* in Kiyooka's work. Its "inspiration can be traced to such prosaic sources as a neon sign seen through the slats of a bamboo blind, the moving pattern of shadows on his studio floor, or an oval panel of bevelled plate glass in an old West End door" (Macdonald 651). But the oval has also been an important spiritual image symbolizing the *hieros gamos*, or marriage of heaven and earth, and Kiyooka's work is no exception: "Art ain't anything without the sacred" he said in the catalogue to his 1975 retrospective (*Kiyooka*). In the same catalogue, Bowering acknowledged the craftsmanship and high finish in the artist's work – neither of which is adequately conveyed in the imperfect reproductions in *El Corno Emplumado* – as existential unrest come to centre. In this sense, the virtually omnipresent letters in the *El Corno* collages may be the remnants of a poisoned language, but they could also be the stuttering or questioning beginnings of a new speech, as in "RRSSSTTTTTUU", "Do you have to be asked?" or Kiyooka's daughter's "scrawl with a felt-tip pen" (Kiyooka to Bowering, Bowering papers NLC).

The collages conclude with an allusion to the Mexican context of the volume, an image quite different from the preceding ones in composition, tonality and subject-matter: like an inverted exclamation mark, a cat is perched atop a tall cactus, fenced in by an equally tall grey mass on either side. She has little space to manoeuvre, but she persists.

CHAPTER THREE

Newspaper Collage: *Rocky Mountain Foot*

Sunday after getting out of the house
twelve oclock of a winter's day:
> the stucco churches
> empty out their
> old women
> & small boys with home haircuts

like the politicians on TV
all rural all interested
in crops & the flag
> built on the new testament
> that is the Scriptures
> converted to piano in the tabernacle
> Sunday sound
> off the brown snow of Seventh Avenue:

> "Hear the message ...
>> EAVESDROPPING
>> ON THE ANGELS
>
> Enjoy the music ...
>> IT'S YOUTH NIGHT
>
> Ministry of Music by our Young People"

I drive past at twelve oclock
my radio tuned to music
of distant Mozart
my eyes indulgent on old women

And they were filled with the
Holy Ghost, and began to speak
with other tongues, as the Spirit gave
them utterance.
> ("calgary downtown sunday," *Rocky Mountain Foot*)

Newspaper Collage: *Rocky Mountain Foot* 41

As an art form which combines objects and materials traditionally considered incompatible, the collage is a particularly appropriate expression of modern urban life: "If [the reader] lives in the city, as most contemporary readers do, he is living in a collage ... a laundromat will be flankt by a Greek restaurant & a Chinese curio shoppe. Where unlike things are stuck together they create a new reality. With the reader's help" (1982 b: 121-122).

Rocky Mountain Foot: a lyric, a memoir (1968) does experiment with different types of print, but instead of seeking the collaboration of a visual artist as in *The Man in Yellow Boots,* Bowering translated the collage into its literary equivalent, namely a juxtaposition of heterogeneous texts. This juxtaposition begins, probably inadvertently, with the packaging of the book, for one wonders if the authors who produced the promotional text for *Rocky Mountain Foot* were aware of its ironical dissonance with the poems. "Seasons and regions ... sun and snow ... pioneers and entrepreneurs ... premiers and Indians ... tourists and cities ... Rocky Mountains and Lake Louise ... all these make up Alberta ... and all these make up *Rocky Mountain Foot*" (1968 n.p.) – this blurb hardly prepares the reader for the often sharply satirical poems in which Alberta is described as "the community / of God, the commonality / of the slipt disc" ("geopolitic"). Nor does the aerial view of stylized prairie fields or cities on the cover anticipate the "patchwork of squares, / skin disease with roads" ("alberta"). The biographical sketch on the cover establishes Bowering's Albertan pedigree: "His grandfather was a circuit-rider who travelled south of Edmonton ... George Bowering taught for two years at the University of Calgary, where he came to know the peculiar charm and beauty of Alberta." However, the poems sharply attack "the hate-belching preachers" ("the plain"), and there is a constant undercurrent of longing for the Coast: "This is Calgary, yes, / winter is over, yes, the sea is far away" ("spring rime in Calgary"). The author's photograph is the same as the one used in *Mirror on the Floor,* but it eliminates the jagged, self-referential tear along the edge that appears there. Yet the poems show Bowering even less convinced of his authorial supremacy than in previous collections, and in "old snow in the new year" he sketches a parody of himself growing fat and lethargic in a basement suite, "watching the murk / of television / blue bulge reflected off black window / dark blowy snow outside / wants in."

Clearly the publishers intended to profit from the popular interest in local history spawned by the Centennial by publicizing the book – anything but a collection of regionalist verse – as a travel poster and history textbook. At the same time, the promoters provided an ironic parallel to the many conflicts between official and poetic discourse exposed in *Rocky*

Mountain Foot. Besides a suite of poems, the book contains clippings from "*The Imperial Oil Review, Our Alberta* (printed by Calgary Power Ltd.), *The Badlands of the Red Deer River* (Printed by the Dominion of Canada), *The Frank Slide Story* by Frank Anderson, *The Calgary Albertan, The Calgary Herald*, Program Notes of the Calgary Film Society & the poems of some Canadian poets" (1968a: 127). One poem, "colonel fleming et jules et jim," consists entirely of a "cut-up of a letter written by the chief film censor of the Province of Alberta" (100). For much of the book, the clippings are reproduced in a distinctive print and are instantly recognizable as "extraneous" matter, but half-way through the volume poems in cursive print begin to assume the place of the clippings. In "odd lost sounds," "without words," "an old conceit," "footprints, fenceposts," "warm february," "the blood red fuck," "prairie music," and "mud-time," the juxtaposition is not so much between poem and clipping, as between different poetic voices, possibly versions of the same voice.

In the Bayard / David interview, Bowering describes the collage as a way to avoid the subjectivism of the lyric: "I don't know what the model might have been but I had a sense that the way to do that was to inject or meet what you were writing with the other ... that there will be something like a collaboration perhaps" (Bayard, David 98). Like Robert Duncan, Bowering had become increasingly suspicious of the selectivity, solipsism and potential social irresponsibility of the lyric, and like Duncan, he generally refused, from *Rocky Mountain Foot* onwards, to "write the perfect lyric," but instead felt he "must corrupt the linear melody for the strategy of the collage, bring up thematic unity with elements recalcitrant and untamed, and bring in contemporary horrors" (Weatherhead 174).[1] Revealingly, *Rocky Mountain Foot* appeared in the same year as *The Gangs of Kosmos*, which, although still mostly composed of lyrics, relinquished the metaphors of flower and dance central to *The Man in Yellow Boots* and *The Silver Wire* for a pervasive tone of disillusionment and a feeling of isolation (see, for example, "A Comment on the Singular," "The House," "The Silence" "Now You," "Our Triple Birth").

Bowering asserts that he does not "know what the model might have been," but there are a number of strong possibilities, Williams' *Paterson* foremost among them, as well as Whitman's *Leaves of Grass*, Ginsberg's *Howl*, and Olson's *Maximus Poems*. The TISH collective mined *Paterson* for ideas and quotations, and among the results were Davey's series of poems "no ideas but in things," Bowering's essay "Dance to a Measure," and the interview between Author and Canadian Tradition in *Another Mouth*. In *Rocky Mountain Foot*, Bowering goes beyond such isolated references and uses *Paterson* as a model for the overall structure of the book.

Newspaper Collage: *Rocky Mountain Foot*

Paterson, a long poem in five books published between 1946 and 1958, is a collage poem incorporating excerpts from letters, local history, biographies, newspaper articles, interviews, scholarly books, street signs, statistics, inventories. Alternating with Williams' poetry, these passages, which range from the scientific to the banal, re-enact the major principles of dadaist collage and ready-mades. Because they continually interrupt the sequence of the poems, the clippings sabotage a unified point-of-view. Instead, the clippings suggest a chorus of divergent but simultaneous voices among which the poems do not appear to be singularly privileged. The traditional separation between "high" and "low" art, between documentary, scientific, and poetic discourses is effectively questioned, a procedure for which Bowering, through Olson and Whitehead, claims to have found a model in quantum physics. Here, "the same laws describe phenomena in any co-ordinate system so a law perceived by an observer can be translated into any frame of reference" and "Any coordinate system is equivalent to any other and no one system has any particular claim to finality" (Perry 207).

Rocky Mountain Foot re-enacts a specific form of collage, the newspaper (Bollard), whose design Williams considered particularly symptomatic of modernist – and American – discourse, for a poem should contain "the same materials as newsprint, the same dregs" (Williams 295). On a typical front page, headlines and stories of vastly different content and origin will be placed next to each other, often in fragmented form (to be continued on another page or in another issue), and their individual rank will be determined by news-worthiness only, an interrelationship Bowering explored in several of the political poems in *The Man in Yellow Boots*. Occasionally he casts himself or his characters as passive receivers and consumers of the news; in *Concentric Circles*, for instance, the characters seem to drown in discarded piles of the "San Francisco *Chronicle*, the Washington *Post*. Bombay *Gazette*" (Bowering 1977a: 9). But the unexpected connections between the ordinary and extraordinary in newspapers and other media like radio and television also often jolt the poet into a sharper awareness of his social responsibility as a writer (and parent): in "April 25, 1972" (*Another Mouth*), he juxtaposes his crawling baby daughter with the television image of an astronaut, and in *At War With the U.S.*, vignettes of Thea's first year are interwoven with reflexions on 1973 news items:

August 15, 1973, a day, they say
for the future. The B-52s are ordered
to stop dumping on Cambodia

My last day in the Greek neighbourhood

As he points out in his essay "Modernism Could not Last Forever" (1982b), Bowering even perceives an allegory of postmodernism as a whole in the accidental super-imposition of television image and perceiver's reflection.

In *Rocky Mountain Foot*, Bowering elevates the writer's role as social conscience to that of prophet and iconoclast. In so doing, he adopts the stance of the new prophets whose arrival Whitman – like Shelley and Emerson before him – announced in the Preface to the 1855 edition of *Leaves of Grass*, a text which also provided Bowering with a title for his book *The Gangs of Kosmos*:

There will soon be no more priests. The work is done. They may wait awhile ... perhaps a generation or two ... dropping off by degrees. A superior breed shall take their place ... the gangs of Kosmos and prophets en masse shall take their place.... Through the divinity of themselves shall the Kosmos and the new breed of poets be interpreters of men and women and of all events and things. They shall find their inspiration in real objects today, symptoms of the past and future. (Whitman xi)

The poem "the crumbling wall" which, in *The Man in Yellow Boots*, mostly functions as a metapoetic statement, here becomes a battle-cry later enforced by another in "odd lost sounds":

... *Write! Write! break a hole*
in the wall with
it, a poem

This hortatory voice emerges with particular strength and effectiveness in poems which juxtapose the geometrical severity of Calgary's grid-system with nature's energy and exuberance. "above calgary" opens with compact, squarish stanzas imitating a city-block:

The paper shows me
aerial photographs of Calgary,
great handful of boxes
dropt by God, arranged
in squares by contractors

However, the poet envisages how the "box people" inhabiting this city are released into an ecstatic riot of colours and shapes, and the stanzas dissolve into a series of long lines, imperatives and exclamations in which the echo of Whitman's biblical rhetoric is apparent, as is the resonance of Ginsberg's apocalyptic vision of the "Moloch" in *Howl*.

Drop confetti of God on their rooftops!
Let ten million groundhogs heap dirt in their driveways!

Make the television dance curlicue schottisches across the
      patio puddles!
...
Churches bulge at the seams with gaily changing love-girls
      & love-boys singing oceanic denunciations of
      desert dust & city planning!

Here, Bowering re-enacts the opposition of "marriage" and "divorce," central concepts in *Paterson*, where "divorce" denotes the separation of man from nature's things and "marriage," his humble and joyful co-existence with them. Williams focused on the Passaic Waterfalls to illustrate the continuum of life. In *Rocky Mountain Foot*, the prairies and its people – "web-footed for the sea" ("calgary") – seem to be dreaming of the pre-historic ocean which covered their land, but more often than not they have to make do with" [a] thin trickle of water" which "cuts thru cow country mud" ("vancouver-courtenay-calgary"). The poet's own longing for the "Coast where shells / sprout out of the water" and where "on the edge the shoes move, / in the dance of people piling / on people" ("back in vancouver for a vancouver visit") is also the longing of the land to be liberated from bondage:

the city itself re-arranged in looney-tune rib tickle of
      pure chance, automobiles suiciding in Bow River
      & Elbow River, laughing in their hysterical death
  ("above calgary")

"above calgary" describes a fantastic vision, but every year the "mud-time" of spring run-off, the cracking of the frozen river, and the emergence of flowers and grass all join in a real liberation, "the concert of bravery and beauty in the animal world and the vegetable world" (Bowering 1985: 80). In "the grass," a poem as tightly packed as frozen ground except for the last line, new vegetation emerges from the melting soil "like a sea-lion coming/ out of water." Alberta sharpened Bowering's understanding of the "locus;" many of the poems in *Rocky Mountain Foot* read like an echo of Olson's *Maximus Poems,* more specifically of Sam Perry's celebratory reading of them in TISH 10:

The water is drawn from and floats its mother earth and saps through all Okeanos, is part of all the earth ... all things grown live on water and earth and all things living die and return to earth and water. Maximus carries this scheme inland, aware of the water, conscious of the forces that mould, he walked among the tossed boulders of Dogtown seeping into the earth digging his self into the earth to sense what passions formed that particular dust. (Perry 208)

The continuum of life and the poet's place in it are central issues in *Rocky Mountain Foot* and, ironically, they are particularly apparent in the features which allowed McClelland and Stewart to advertise the book as a collection of patriotic and descriptive verse. Superficially speaking, *Rocky Mountain Foot* is a sequence of loosely connected travel episodes, initiated by the poet's journey from the coast to Calgary through the Rockies and the foothills, concluded by a return visit to Vancouver. His stance is frequently that of a tourist who not only coolly observes that "Lake Louise looks / just like her pictures" ("the religious lake"), but also collects the kind of random information found in guidebooks, on the dinosaurs ("albertasaurus"), the origin of place-names ("history is us," "the name"), the cultural contribution of the oriental population ("east to west") and eccentric newspaper editors ("the calgary eye-opener"). Often, the poet's view is remarkably detached, as when he drives through downtown Calgary, his "car radio tuned to music / of distant Mozart / [his] eyes indulgent on old women" ("calgary downtown sunday"), or on the many other occasions when he observes the land from a moving car or flying airplane ("the oil," "zing," "over the rockies," "above montana," "spinning," "the weight," "harpo, a living stone," "the streets of calgary," "stampede"). His superiority and detachment seem guaranteed, particularly in a poem like "mount norquay," with its obtrusive use of the first person singular which is underlined by parallel construction and indented print: "I am standing under the chairlift," "I look up," "If I look at the sky," " I sit on stump & look down slash," "I lower my head," "I put it at base of stanchion," "I leave the trail," and so on. But on looking at these poems more closely, the reader discovers that the poet's almost continuous motion signifies anything but detached superiority and that the omnipresence of the "I" does not imply control. Commenting on bp Nichol's "Trans-Continental," Bowering explains "We have ... a continuous present, the train on which Einstein's relativistic passenger is justified in believing that he is sitting still, but which is in constant movement as Heraclitus told us all, like a creek we cannot step into twice" (Bowering 1986a: 11). The perceiver, then, is stripped of his Cartesian vision; sometimes he deludes himself into thinking it persists, but accidents like "[spinning] in the Volkswagen / on sudden ice" remind him that

it could be me
swinging on this icy road
in the middle of the Rockies,
it could be the mountains
coming to squeeze me.
    ("spinning")

Newspaper Collage: *Rocky Mountain Foot*

In "the oil," the perceiver's glance, and the lines with it, travel to the right and left, catching glimpses of what there is to see on the highway, but the repetition of "Cadillac" erodes the sense of a reliable concept of perspective:

Now a
    Cadillac, I see a
        nother Cadillac, & there
is the black straight road, &
        a Cadillac,
            two Cadillacs
on the road, racing, North,
        the mountains to the left
blurred by a passing
        Cadillac.

In an essay on Edward Dorn's *Slinger* (1975), Michael Davidson calls the "I" an anachronism, the "last vestige of the self-conscious, rationalizing ego" (447). The "I/eye" in "mount norquay" is apparently left to survey the scene in a more leisurely fashion than the driver on the Alberta highway, yet the poet's glance travels over nothing but debris scattered across the mountainside: peanuts, "one cigar in plastic holder," "one bottle opener," "candy bar wrappers," a penny, a letter. Surveying these random items forces a restless, jerky motion on the perceiver's glance, which makes his stance even more precarious, for "If I look at the sky, I'll fall backward down the hill."

A similar vertigo is instilled in the poet's explorations of local history. In "history is us," Bowering explores a series of place-names. He begins by dispassionately listing etymological notes, but soon adds critical commentary in parentheses: "(So history again / is death)," "(or rather, history / is past.)." Legend, usually considered a form of myth, and therefore exempted from historical critique, is here included in the analysis:

Medicine Hat, Alberta
        where serpent told Cree
        brave to throw
        his wife
        into the water

        which he did
        for power &
        an old man's hat

        to kill the Blackfoot.

The poem concludes by punning on the word "proper" in "proper names" which can be said to mean both "neat, schematic" (as in a map) and "pertaining to property,"

> which is
> another name for
> history.

"history is us" weaves back and forth on the page in a skeptical statement-and-question pattern insisting on conditionals ("if names are history") and alternatives ("or rather, history / is past," "Or it could be said"). The conclusion is presented as an afterthought and formulated as a series of discrete phrases abruptly separated by periods.

This halting progress differs sharply from the smoothly composed historical texts quoted in excerpts throughout the book, as in

> Father Lacombe's adventurous life in the west was filled with colourful scenes: riding full-tilt across the prairies; running his dogsled, his black robe tucked into deerskin pants; sometimes almost starving and freezing while he laboured for Christianity and the welfare of the Alberta Indians, (27)

or in

> The grim cascade of limestone from Turtle Mountain will undoubtedly lie like an enormous scar across the beautiful Crow's Nest Valley for centuries to come. The great tombstone is probably the most awe-inspiring in the world and stands as a constant reminder of those 100 seconds of wind, rock and dust which wrote the epic of Frank Slide in indelible limestone, shale and coal script. (44)

Both texts are dominated by metaphors placing man, or more precisely, the white man, at the centre of the universe: Father Lacombe is cast in the role of a latter-day knight conquering the vicissitudes of a harsh climate to reach his holy grail, that is the conversion of the Indians; Turtle Mountain is both anthropomorphized ("an enormous scar") and presented as a book for man to read. The differences of these texts with "history is us" are particularly striking in formulations which appear to be identical with Bowering's linguistic strategies in the poem, namely the insistent use of the participle of the present in the first text and the qualifier "probably the most awe-inspiring" in the second. The latter, of course, is only a rhetorical marker not at all meant to imply insecurity in the speaker, but prudence at most. And the participle of the present does not suggest the Einsteinian disorientation in time and space usually associated with it in Bowering's poetry, but instead conveys an intensely purposeful sense of direction

Newspaper Collage: *Rocky Mountain Foot* 49

which conquers all obstacles. Thus, the participle only serves as a dynamic counterpoint to the past tense which summarizes the results of Father Lacombe's spiritual journey ("starving and freezing while he laboured for Christianity and the welfare of the Alberta Indians").

As an alternative to conventional history, Bowering proposes archaeology, the patient recovery of layers of sediment, which, in their physical appearance, resemble the paratactic structures with which he experiments in "history is us" and other poems. Several of the pieces in *Rocky Mountain Foot*, both poems and clippings, allude to fragmented remnants: teeth, footprints, coprolites. Nor are such findings restricted to long-extinct dinosaurs, but, since "history is us," Bowering includes man (and himself) in his archaeological search. His traces are neither more nor less distinct than those of his fellow creatures:

Footprint in the snow. Cut clean,
½ inch lower than snow,
                    weight
of an old body, down leg,
                    impression
in snow ...
...
How many footprints have I made?
        Any impression on the wind?
    ("the mark")

Rocky Mountain Foot appeared in 1968, after Bowering had left Calgary to begin a doctorate on Shelley at the University of Western Ontario, a project interrupted a year later for a position as writer-in-residence at Sir George Williams University in Montreal. Although he made important contacts in London with the painters and poets who had started a "scene" there which is often compared to that of sixties' Vancouver, he strongly disagreed with them on one issue – the concept of regionalism. *Rocky Mountain Foot* and another suite of poems published shortly after, *George, Vancouver: A Discovery Poem* (1970), may be called his poetic manifestos on the subject, the essays "Why James Reaney is a Better Poet" (1968) and "Reaney's Region" (1983) his critical ones. In the latter, Bowering declares his affinity with the London artists' concern with place, but distances himself from their interpretation of it. He suspected "regionalism" of perpetuating the grid-system that had dismayed him in Alberta, for both imply man's ascendancy over nature. He particularly blamed Northrop Frye for promoting poetry with a mythopoeic direction, in which man, says Bowering, treats nature "as organizer and possessor of it" (Bowering 1968: 27). Ontario's strong sense of tradition seemed ample proof that such control was not about to be relinquished:

The word "region" implies rulers, as regents, regimes, even rajahs, all those regal authorities who reign over reichs. The word finds itself in adjectives or verbs such as correct and direct and erect, and especially right. Regis designates a straight line, especially a boundary, of property, for instance, or of a county. (38)

"Locus," by contrast, posits the poet as "[reshaper] of an environment by virtue of [his] entry into it" (48). *George, Vancouver*, a poem employing a similar collage technique as *Rocky Mountain Foot* in order to place the European conqueror's discourse next to the indigenous language of the land, evokes the west coast to describe such an entry: the edge joining water and land is "completely clean / completely free of death" (Bowering 1970b: 14). In *Rocky Mountain Foot*, Bowering borrowed Ginsberg's rhapsodic voice to conjure up the openness he associated with the coast; when he left London, he translated his response to the scene there into similar verse:

I take leave, worship not your heroes, count me out,
disallow trading stamps, pave the streets, paint the Baptist Church,
break the strikes, pay the cops, collect the parking fees,
fill the rice crispies box with blue plastic airplanes,
elect good music radio stations, show me the toe of your boot,

goodbye, I'm away again, never settled as you are....
  ("Goodbye Middlesex County," *Seventy-One Poems for People*)

CHAPTER FOUR

Bowering and the London Scene

I see the sun's crystal corners
dull & rounded by Niagara's deep chimneys
of burnt bones.
        The Great Lakes
with their beaches of dead fish.
Small parks with men at the gates
looking for blue money
from the insides of cars.

Ontario's heroes have the names of cities
along the asphalt roads.
    (from "Goodbye Middlesex County"
    [for Owen Curnoe], *Alphabet*)

1. *"Swinging London"*

Despite Bowering's reservations about the ideological orientation of the London artists, he also found much in common with them. The fact that his sardonic poem "Goodbye Middlesex County" was first published in Reaney's "Kindergarten *Alphabet*" (Mayne 58) indicates that he found an open-minded and generous community there. Occasionally, he even allowed himself to be identified with the very immersion in regionalism and myth he denounced elsewhere. Thus, one reads with considerable amusement a report in which Ross Woodman, professor of English at the University of Western Ontario and indefatigable chronicler of the London scene, numbers Bowering among its foremost artists at the show of the London Art Museum entitled "Cultural Heritage of this Region":

On the closing night of this show, a group of London artists gathered to read from their own work. Taking up positions within the beam frames of the various exhibits superbly assembled from all over Southern Ontario, they looked as much a part of the 'cultural heritage' as the objects themselves. There they sat – James Reaney,

Colleen Thibaudeau, Jack Chambers, Greg Curnoe, George Bowering, Ron Bates – like carven images, and when they rose to read their voices sounded at once contemporary and ancestral. And their words, it seemed, were as regionally rooted as the objects. (Woodman 1967 n.p.)

As in Vancouver, the flowering of the London art scene occurred mainly during the Centennial decade, but almost from the beginning its artists were more politically oriented and organized than their counterparts on the west coast, who, for the most part, worked harmoniously within existing structures such as the university and the art gallery. The politicization of Canadian art which Bowering witnessed among his colleagues in London may have provided him with important models for his own growing involvement in various activities of the Canada Council. His extensively documented advisory functions show him to be a shrewd negotiator for the rights of the writer (Bowering papers NLC). Like Jack Chambers, who, after discovering that he was terminally ill, instructed his dealer to raise the price of his work, Bowering considers artistic integrity not incompatible with a sound business sense.

The beginning of the London "scene" is generally associated with 1962, when a "happening" at the London Art Gallery featuring local artists and guests from Toronto (Michael Snow, Joyce Wieland, Michel Lambert, and Michel Sanouillet) initiated a series of controversial and iconoclastic activities designed to challenge the tyranny of established cultural institutions. In 1966, artists protested the LAG curator's prudish decision to exclude John Boyle's *Seated Nude* from a show: they removed their own works as well and made a well-publicized event of it. This éclat was followed by the removal, in 1969, of Greg Curnoe's mural from "the walls of the international airways concourse at Dorval airport ... because of the mural's alleged anti-Vietnam, anti-American content" (Poole 141), an incident which only served to fuel public interest in Curnoe's work and ideas and provided welcome publicity for the travelling exhibition *The Hart of London* arranged by the National Gallery of Canada. At approximately the same time, a letter from the National Gallery requesting Chambers's permission to include reproductions of his work in a slide set for schools and colleges set off yet another controversy, for Chambers refused to sign over copyrights, invited artists across the country to join him in his protest, and, based on the strong support he received, founded the "Canadian Artists Representation" (CAR) to protect artists' rights (Poole 142). Most of these scandals had practical consequences: CAR successfully bargained for a 'fair exchange' in fees or purchases from public galleries and museums"

(Poole 143); and the incident surrounding the *Seated Nude* is, by some, held responsible for the opening of 20/20 Gallery, an alternative, cooperative venture that succeeded Curnoe's more emphatically regionalist Region Gallery (1962-63).

20/20 Gallery was also interdisciplinary, comparable to Vancouver's Intermedia, and Bowering found the cooperation among painters and poets and the general interest in multi-media approaches very congenial: in London, he introduced David McFadden and Greg Curnoe to each other, later collaborators on *The Great Canadian Sonnet* (1970, 1971) and *Animal Spirits: Stories to Live By* (1983). A particularly outlandish undertaking which brought together some of London's foremost artists was the "Nihilist Spasm Band," featuring Murray Favro, Greg Curnoe, and others, who played on home-made instruments, "long, loud, bell-mouth kazoos, a kind of slide clarinet that squeaks, an electric guitar of eccentric design, and a whacking amplified bass that makes the glasses shake on the tabletops" (Lord 1968: 19f.). Typically, the Nihilist Spasm Band had its origin in a political event, the 1962 Ontario provincial election, when Favro and friends created the Nihilist Party, an Ontario counterpart to Jacques Ferron's Rhinoceros Party.

Compared to the Nihilist Spasm Band's chaotic antics, the collaboration among playwrights, poets and artists appears positively idyllic: Greg Curnoe designed marionettes and sets for James Reaney's *Little Red Riding Hood,* and he also provided the marionettes for Reaney's *Apple Butter,* while Chambers created the sets. Chambers moreover contributed eerily pointillist drawings to Reaney's *The Dance of Death at London* (1963). *The Dance of Death* first appeared in Reaney's publication *Alphabet: A Semiannual Devoted to the Iconography of the Imagination* (1960-1971), a rich source for the close interaction among Canadian poets and painters and for multiple talents like George Johnston whose poem "Honey" was reproduced in the author's elaborate calligraphy and with his intricate drawings. Although Greg Curnoe denounced *ARTSCANADA* for its American orientation, this publication contributed to disseminating Reaney's ideas to a larger audience, after Anne Brodzky, education officer at the London Art Gallery since 1965, became the editor. Following her appointment, the London scene received regular and extensive national coverage, often written by local critics. Bowering may have been bemused by the contrast with the situation in Vancouver, where activities and ideas did not have access to as powerful a forum, and where the quality of the documentation was often woefully out of proportion with that of the activities in galleries and lecture-halls.

In the Bayard/David interview, Bowering calls the writing he did in London "just hopeless," but he does acknowledge the impact local painters had on his ideas, Greg Curnoe and Jack Chambers in particular (Bayard,David 88), artists whose friendship carried over into their work: Chambers's film *R-34* focuses on Curnoe, and his painting *Sunday Morning No. 2* includes a *trompe-l'oeil* rendition of a canvas by Curnoe, while Curnoe included Chambers in his Dorval mural as well as dedicating an elegiac work to him. Their *oeuvre* sharpened Bowering's sense for the interaction of the personal and the public, and moved it onto a new plane. Deprived of the intimate sense of a place with which British Columbia and even Alberta had provided him, he "began to look elsewhere, inward, as they say, & into my personal time, around me in dreams" (Bowering 1974c: 8) and experimented with forms of life-writing, *Autobiology* (1972a) foremost among them. At the same time, Bowering's writing began to move toward an emphatic acknowledgement of his double role as teacher and writer, a development of which *A Short Sad Book* (1977) is arguably the most important document. The latter is ostentatiously connected to Curnoe's convictions, while *Autobiology* may be usefully compared to Chambers's work.

2. Greg Curnoe and A Short Sad Book

Curnoe and Bowering's friendship is extensively documented in their works: Curnoe provided covers for two of Bowering's books and for 1989 ECW's special issue on Bowering, and Curnoe's name spooks through several of Bowering's poems (*Uncle Louis*, "Goodbye Middlesex County," *Kerrisdale Elegies*) as well as appearing in the dedications of *Layers 1-13* (1973) and *Another Mouth* (1979). Bowering was also one of a three-man crew who helped to mount Curnoe's Dorval mural. Their friendship carries over into an affinity in intention and style, expressed most obviously in their shared fascination with the popular and the banal. Curnoe's self-portrait of the painter as bicycle racer (*Self-Portrait, 20-24 June, 1980*) could easily be exchanged for the photograph of Bowering as baseball player adorning the cover of *Books in Canada* (November 1987), or for his many literary self-portraits in that role. Both have been praised for the encyclopedic inclusiveness of their work (Kamboureli 1985; Nemiroff) and have won impressive recognition from the establishment: Bowering has received two Governor General's Awards, and Curnoe was the sole artist chosen to represent Canada at the 37th Biennale in Venice. Both, however, have also been criticized for the "jock dimension" (Fitzgerald n.p.) in their work which has led critics time and again to declare Curnoe and Bowering marginal, even delinquent. The scandal periodically incited by their work only seems to confirm this opinion: Louis Dudek's response to the eroticism in *The Silver Wire* corresponds to the offense caused by Curnoe's *24 Hourly Notes* at the 1968 International Edinburgh Festival, where three panels were censored as obscene; and the "Dorval Mural Affair" bears strong resemblance to the outrage provoked by *Burning Water*.

But the marginal has always been a deliberate choice for Bowering and Curnoe. In his catalogue for the 1982 Curnoe retrospective at the National Gallery, Paul Théberge used *Drawer Full of Stuff* (1961) as an emblem of Curnoe's work as a whole (Théberge 1982: 5). The items collected in the drawer – bus tickets, a dinky toy, a table spoon, Sunlight soap, a double socket with plug, a bicycle chain, and others – are fragments of everyday life, but, assembled in a frame, they are granted exceptional status. Similarly, a collage created after a visit to Expo '67, entitled *Bowering Westmount No. 4* because Curnoe stayed in the Bowerings' Montreal apartment, collects trivia picked up on the site of the exhibition, much as Kiyooka's photographs *StoneDgloves* recorded workers' gloves trampled underfoot at the World Fair in Osaka. Not surprisingly, Curnoe's esthetics are grounded in Dadaism. In the late fifties, the literary historian Michel Sanouillet had increased his interest in the work of Eluard, Aragon, Tzara and Breton, and in 1961, Curnoe participated with Michael Snow, Joyce Wieland and Gordon Rayner in the Neo-Dada exhibition organized by Avrom Isaacs.

Curnoe's focus on the marginal and, in the case of *Bowering Westmount No. 4*, on the refuse generated by grandiose national self-display, corresponds to his protest against the predominance of metropolitan art centres and of artists lionized by the critics; like Bowering, he champions alternative artists and establishments. His participation in the Biennale notwithstanding, Curnoe's loyalties are often aggressively local: he refuses to show his work in New York, challenges Picasso's role as "the world's greatest artist" because he "was another Imperial Centre" (Hale 12), and, instead, collects Canadian soft drink bottles; he is co-founder of the Association for the Documentation of Neglected Aspects of Culture in Canada, and he objected to the University of Western Ontario's acquisition of manuscripts by Milton for a quarter of a million dollars, while the historic core of Curnoe's home town was in danger of being replaced by parking lots and office buildings.

Because Curnoe's political and esthetic convictions are so emphatically grounded in the local and personal, they appealed to Bowering, who, particularly after his acquaintance with the editors of *El Corno Emplumado*, had become increasingly wary of American political and cultural predominance, but found it equally impossible to identify with the propagation of Canadian heroes and icons in the wake of the Centennial. Curnoe's approach, passionately pro-Canadian but never dogmatic, offered a welcome alternative. Both men felt that the uncritical installation of cultural symbols could undermine their country's national awakening. For nationalist symbols often perpetuate the very imperialism they pretend to exorcise because they lean heavily toward the stereotypical and exotic, and while seemingly abolishing one power relation, they serve as the alibi for another. Joyce Wieland recognized this danger when she pointed toward the sexism inherent in popular allegories of the land in her bronze sculptures, *The Spirit of Canada Suckles the French and English Beavers* and in *Bear and 'Spirit of Canada'* (1970-71), in which a bear is seen to mount a spread-eagled female. An even sharper ambiguity emerges from Wieland's comment that making *Reason and Passion,* a film depicting a cross-Canada journey with Trudeau as representative of all Canadians, made her feel like "Leni Riefenstahl" (Lippard 3).

Published a decade after the Centennial, *A Short Sad Book* outlines the author's change of attitude towards his country: "I love this country, I didn't then, thirty years ago" (Bowering 1977c: 15). Later, he includes one of his literary mentors in this *volte-face:* "Well, here I am Walt, & I dont see you around & you still havent annex'd Cuba & Kanada" (26). At the same time, however, Bowering resists the "culture-fixing" (Davey 1983a: 5) which often accompanies attempts at national self-definition, and his text sabotages the easy equations he found offensive in Northrop Frye and Margaret Atwood's criticism. Throughout *A Short Sad Book,* there are grammatical, semantic, and morphemic slippages, but, as in *Rocky Mountain Foot,* the strongest displacements occur in proper reference, generic references, and personal pronouns. When "Victor" dissolves into "Vic d'Or," "art" assumes the identity of "Art," and "Evangeline" is transformed into "Evange" (*alter ego* of Bowering's wife Angela, a feisty presence in *A Short Sad Book*), then it is only logical that the narrator's "I" too should become fluid. In "I love this country. I didn't then thirty years ago but am I I" (52), the first-person pronoun suddenly looks like the Roman numeral for the number "two." The obsessive search for a cultural identity and a unifying myth which characterizes Canadian thematic criticism becomes a futile endeavour indeed if the subject itself cannot be trusted to remain stable. *A Short Sad Book* is an encyclopedia of deconstructed cultural myths, but one particularly effective demolition occurs in Bowering's response to the geographical myth, specifically the dichotomies believed to exist between North and South, West and East. A popular definition of Canada's identity consists in mythologizing its geography, including the dichotomies believed to exist between North and South, West and East. As if swiftly cruising about in an airplane, the narrator establishes that "We say back east & back east they say down east & back east & down east they say out west" (22) and "In the north in Inuvik they told me they get out for a while & then they want to go back, into the north" (23). While magisterially surveying Canada's geography and the idioms used to describe its inhabitants' relation to it, however, the narrator also undermines his own, presumably reliable, outlook. The syntax in the first quotation is ambiguous, because the ampersands may be understood as either linking several main clauses ("We say back east [;] & back east they say down east [;] & back east & down east they say out west") or several direct objects ("We say back east & back east [;] they say down east & back east & down east [;] they say out west"). Instead of following the printed line sequentially, the reader's eye moves back and forth seeking to establish the logical ordering of the sentence, an effort further undermined by the insistent repetition of words, sounds, structures. The second version makes less "sense" than the first, but, like a ritualistic chant or political slogan, it has a hypnotic logic of its own.

Thus, Bowering partly achieves his effect by playing two different rhythms, one generated by traditional syntax, the other by sound, against each other. In his panel series *True North Strong and Free, Nos. 1-5* (1968), Curnoe pursues a similar technique. Each panel bears rubber-stamped inscriptions. Although most of these can be deciphered ("Canada Feeds the Brain!" "Close the 49th Parallel etc," "Canada Costs Less Than Drugs," "Canada Always Loses!" "And Did Chartier Die in Vain??"), the messages appear fragmented by their separation into individual panels, the rubber-stamps used to print the slogans are faded, and the words are distorted almost out of recognition by their arrangement within the panel. At first sight, for instance, the fourth panel reads like a cryptic message in Spanish: "Canad a alwa ys los es!" Here, the medium used helps to defamiliarize the words. At the same time, it endows them with new vigour, for a tired phrase now functions as a secret code. Moreover, because the words are crowded into narrow panels, the slogans appear like excerpts from larger, more complex statements, and the "etc" at the end of the "Close the 49th Parallel" may be read not as an expression of apathy or exasperation, but as a signal for plans of action being formed.

In *True North Strong and Free*, Curnoe intended to revive nationalist slogans, not necessarily ironize them, but in his "Amendments" to John

Boyle's *Refus continental,* Curnoe's approach closely resembles Bowering's burlesque; this approach has caused Curnoe's admirers some bewilderment, most notably the Marxist critic Barry Lord, who considers the "Amendments" a frivolous aberration and suggests that *Map of North America* (1972) and *True North Strong and Free* (1968) are a clearer expression of Curnoe's convictions (Lord 1974). But Curnoe, although he heartily endorsed Boyle's condemnation of American political and cultural predominance, was also enough of a Dadaist to be wary of the potential absurdities of *all* political dogma. The "Amendments" recommend "closing the Canada-U.S. border – even to birds, insects, and germs; he demanded that Coca-Cola be banned in Canada, that jazz and rock be prohibited; that American art in Canada be exhibited as degenerate and auctioned off in the United States; that radio station CKNW play nothing but 'O Canada' twenty-four hours a day – except Sunday, reserved for 'The Maple Leaf Forever'" (Théberge 20). Cloaked in the diction of assertive nationalism, the "Amendments" bristle with allusions to earlier occasions, where such language became the instrument of indiscriminate oppression, thus duplicating the very power constellation the language had set out to destroy. Curnoe, a jazz connaisseur who taught Bowering "a lot about contemporary jazz" (Bowering 1979b: 105), knew only too well that "jazz" and "rock" may have originated in the United States, but that they also significantly subverted racist and conservative attitudes in that country and elsewhere. The word "degenerate" of course alludes to the Nazis' destruction of unwanted, because explicitly or implicitly critical, works of art and literature, a historical precedent to which Curnoe may have become especially sensitive after the Dorval Mural Affair. The national anthem and other patriotic songs can carry ominous overtones too; both "O Canada" (written and composed by French-Canadians) and "The Maple Leaf Forever" conveyed messages of English domination and unwanted federalism to the Péquistes: in *A Short Sad Book,* Bowering describes a Montreal hockey-game at which Gilles Vigneault's "Mon pays" replaced the anthem. (An additional complication emerged when Québec federalists, following the Péquistes' appropriation of Québec's cultural symbols, *fleur-de-lys* and Vigneault's songs included, seized upon the maple leaf flag and the national anthem as their banner and battle hymn). Curnoe, who makes forays into Quebec folk art, is aware of the tensions barely contained in Canada's seemingly anodyne cultural symbols. On one occasion, he found his own ethnic preconceptions shattered when an old Quebec fiddler refused to be pressed into an anthropological mold, would not give a demonstration of traditional music, and pointed out that he much preferred "modern music, like Robert Charlebois" (Théberge 20).

Likewise, *A Short Sad Book* presents and examines a whole collection of cultural symbols, ranging from historical figures such as Gabriel Dumont, Paul Kane, Van Horne, Ch. G.D. Roberts, Tom Thomson and Louis Riel, to objects and animals, snow, beavers, maple-leaves and moose among them. Each, so the narrator argues, has been co-opted to disguise exploitation – financial, racial, cultural, or sexual: "The maple leaf forever ... There were not many trees with leaves on them. Some of the well-off people in old & big houses had them" (60); "Louis Riel was free but his people were not. Louis Riel died with a T in his hand. It stood for the Toronto Dominion Bank. His people owe a lot of money to the TD bank" (132); "Do they have beavers in British Columbia? I don't believe I have ever seen a beaver. This is getting to be dirtier & dirtier & I cant help it" (72). His years in Montreal made Bowering particularly sensitive to the agricultural myth which had been thrust upon the Québécois by State and Church since the conquest and which was experiencing a curious revival in the works of younger poets: militantly opposed to the reactionary spirit of agriculturalism, they still often seized upon the metaphor of the maternal land to express their nationalist devotion. In chapter XLVI, Stan (editor of Coach House Press) follows the "Pretty Good Canadian Novel ... down the St. Lawrence River." There, he encounters a paragraph which originated in Hugh MacLennan's *Two Solitudes*:

Spring leapt quickly into full summer that year .... The heat simmered in delicate gossamers along the surface of the plain, cloud formations built themselves up thru the mornings & by afternoon they were majestic above the river. The first year shoots of the seeds that had been consecrated on Saint Marc's Day appeared above the soil in the sunshine. (155)

Replete with images of organic growth, allusions to the Christian calendar, and evocations of picturesque scenery, the passage conveys the messianic propaganda which depicted rural life as legitimate and sacred even if the land was not fertile or even plentiful enough to warrant a predominantly agricultural society. Into this scene, Bowering inserts contemporary Québec poems. Disguised as peasants "waving their crude hoes & rakes," the poems come to life, snarling lines of existentialist anguish: "Je n'ai pas de nom, anonyme, je suis anonyme" (156). Because of their pathos, however, these lines corroborate the stilted effect of the prose passage, the more so since, like speech-balloons in a comic-strip, they float up before the backdrop of clouds, "brown, & composed chiefly of iron sulphide." In criticizing the obsession of nationalist criticism with the land, Bowering echoed the concerns of painter Tony Urquhart and Marxist art critic Barry

Lord. Largely in response to the strangle-hold of the Group of Seven on the Canadian art market, both pointed out that, at best, "landscape painting was ... as non-committed in its way as abstract art" and, at worst, "trophy-hunting, in which the artist as hunter goes into the wilds, finds the prize specimen, and returns with it mounted for exhibition in a safe, urban gallery" (Heath 46f.).

In challenging the process of nationalist auto-stereotyping, Bowering and Curnoe not only mimic its microstructures in syntax, diction, and leitmotifs, but also its macrostructures. Foremost among these are monumental forms like the historical and allegorical epic and drama, as well as their counterparts in the fine arts, mural and sculpture. Often commissioned to mark the opening of theatres or to enhance new public buildings, many of these forms experienced a revival during the Centennial decade. Thus, the Québec poet Michèle Lalonde contributed an oratorio entitled *Terre des hommes* to the artistic programme of Expo '67, Reaney's *Colours in the Dark* was given a lavish production at Stratford, and the social commentary of *The Ecstasy of Rita Joe* was all but submerged in the elaborate ballet and music arrangements added for the play's cross-Canada tour. Fittingly, the Department of Transport marked its contributions to the nation's cohesiveness by commissioning or acquiring works of art for major airports, gently admonishing the artists on one occasion "not to include aircraft forms in their proposals for the simple reason that these would date badly" (Gwyn, 213). Accordingly, Kenneth Lochhead's *Flight and its Allegories* and Art Price's *Welcoming Birds* were selected for Gander and Louis Aschambault's exterior screen and freestanding sculpture *Symbol of Flight* for Ottawa. Particularly richly appointed, Dorval boasted wood and metal sculptures, paintings and tapestries by renowned Canadian artists including Inuit carvers, and there were walls of specially designed, hand-glazed tiles.

Such official art has its roots in patriotic projects such as the embellishment of Washington's Library of Congress, the Hôtel de Ville in Paris, or Toronto's old City Hall: all of these undertakings were designed to bring together prominent artists to celebrate their country's essence and existence. Often such projects were laudable in intention and the results remarkable. At the same time, however, it was impossible for many artists in the sixties to endorse the sentiment which had motivated their forebears or to reproduce the forms they had chosen to express it. Rarely had artists been free to depict their own vision: the painters and photographers employed by the Canadian National Railway to record the opening of the West, for instance, were held to create visions of imperialist grandeur suitable for investment publicity and immigration propaganda. Monumental, officially sponsored, art had too often served to legitimize political hegemony, ecological destruction, and social injustice to be taken at face-value, and Canadian artists drew the consequences. If monumental art was to be used at all, then only to expose the hypocrisies of its official versions. Thus, Michèle Lalonde's 1970 "Speak White," a long declamatory piece with specific political allusions, may be read as a reversal of her Expo oratorio; serial poems, Bowering's "George, Vancouver" among them, were often designed to challenge documentary poem and historical epic; and Théâtre Passe Muraille's Brechtian renderings of Canadian history were designed to deconstruct approved cultural heroes and myths.

At their most extreme, such reinterpretations of monumental art provoked official protest and censorship, but in each case, the *éclat* became an integral part of the artist's statement, much as the scandal surrounding Diego Rivera's mural for the Rockefeller Centre brought welcome attention and sparked useful discussion. Curnoe's notorious Dorval panels provided a similar focus of debate. Unlike other Canadian airport art, Curnoe's work did include an air-craft. Besides depicting a full-size 1919 British dirigible and reproducing passages from a German air force commander's diary, the mural displayed images of his son, wife, brother, and cat, and of his friends Jack Chambers, Tony Urquhart and others, most accompanied by their children. Curnoe's two-year-old son Owen appears in the cockpit with the pilot, and in this violent juxtaposition of the personal and the public, Curnoe's artistic creed is encapsulated: "It hit me with full force ... when I put my son in the cockpit. That really shook me" (Reid n.p.). Several years later, Bowering created a similar montage effect in *At War With the U.S.* (1974), for which Curnoe provided a cover drawing (from *The Great Canadian Sonnet*) of a small Canadian airplane shooting down an American fighter; this image serves as a prelude to poems about bringing up a young child in an age of violence. Curnoe's mural ahistorically combined elements from a 1916 text and a 1919 airplane, and he transposed the London / England mentioned in the diary to London / Ontario; also included were a quotation from Mohammed Ali and "a character with a faint resemblance to President Johnson" (quoted in Reid n.p.). In this gigantic collage, history is deprived of its chronological order and myth of its idealizing power, for "Myth is a truth of repetitive time. It is a blot that bleeds thru all time" (Bowering 1977c: 184) and

> History is all about.
> One is in time.
> History is all about.
> Just have a look (98-99).

The airport user travelling past the mural on the escalator must have felt as if he were flying alongside the aircraft and as if he were implicated in its timeless mission, an experience which was a far cry from the sterility of most airport corridors or the tranquillizing *son et lumière* spectacle now being enacted in the corridor connecting two of Chicago's O'Hare terminals. In any event, the impact of Curnoe's mural was too much for too many official visitors. The artist offered to stamp "Censored" on the objectionable parts, but to no avail. It was taken down and removed to storage in the National Gallery. Other, equally sardonic, portraits of contemporary politicians were left alone, probably because they appeared in less sensitive settings: among them are Curnoe's portrait of Mackenzie King, *For Ben Bella* (1964), which was purchased by the Edmonton Art Gallery, and the drawing of W.A.C. Bennett on the cover of *A Short Sad Book*, where the former premier of B.C. is depicted holding Bowering's book and laughing uproariously.

In making his own family and friends the heroes of a mural displayed in a public place and in embodying his personal political views in it, Curnoe violated the unwritten laws to which much of the artwork and literature sponsored by government agencies in the wake of the Centennial was expected to conform: "There are many illustrious episodes in the history of Canada and elsewhere to inspire artistic talent for use in public places," one editorial pointed out; only these were considered "the sort of things taxpayers care to subsidize" (Reid). Yet even had Curnoe produced a work glorifying an approved episode from Canadian history, it is unlikely that his rendition would have met the required criteria. As in his large canvases (the most acclaimed probably being *View of Victoria Hospital, Second Series* [1969-71]), Curnoe used simplified shapes and garish colours in the Dorval panels. Little else seems to be acceptable in official art, however, besides non-referential abstraction or non-committed realism: although John Boyle's work *Our Knell* in the Toronto Queen Street station was executed by one of Canada's most emphatically patriotic artists, the shifting scale and hot pinks and greens in which the mural depicted Nellie McClung and William Lyon Mackenzie King were unsettling to many of its observers. They were quick to suspect parody, and therefore ridicule, of their national past in the mural's defamiliarizing techniques (Lauder). Still, both *Our Knell* and the Dorval mural convinced others that there were important alternatives to the sterility of most official art, and that the interdependence of government funding and art work produced had to be monitored closely.

A Short Sad Book may be called an anti-historical novel, but Bowering

Bowering and the London Scene

has pointed out that the volume is conceived as a large spatial construct resembling a mural. The function of the book is therefore to be as public as Curnoe's work, despite Bowering's casual description of his method:

> I was trying to get the sense of spreading the whole thing out on one big flat surface and then you might see something in the top right-hand corner that connects with something down at the bottom left-hand corner ironically or simply in order to rhyme with it or whatever.... That book just ends because one ran out of space or ran out of pages to do or whatever (Bowering 1979b: 88).

In its seemingly haphazard composition (tell-tale words are "or," "something," "whatever"), *A Short Sad Book* is in contrast with the carefully orchestrated effects of Canada's quintessential historical tableaux, Benjamin West's *The Death of General Wolfe* and its twin *The Death of Montcalm*. Because of their special implications for both English and French, the paintings became *mises en abyme* of national conflict in several sixties and seventies works, ranging from Aquin's *Trou de mémoire* and Léandre Bergeron's comic-strip version of Quebec history, to Laurence's *The Diviners* and Findley's *The Wars* (Ricou 1980/81). Bowering too focuses his concerns in *A Short Sad Book* by referring to these paintings:

> The death of Montcalm & the death of Wolfe were classical in nature.
> They are the most important paintings in Canadian history.
> Wolfe wore red silk & Montcalm wore blue silk & both wore white wigs. Everyone in Canada knows this. (87)

In West's *tableaux*, the observer's eyes are instantly brought to centre on the core group. Wolfe and Montcalm recline in the arms of faithful supporters; their death is given the aura of dignity and sacrifice by alluding, in pose and expression, to the Deposition from the Cross. Soldiers and native allies adopt the roles of decorous extras, the battle-scene itself serves as a decorative backdrop. Colours and shapes are entirely transparent, that is to say they are only significant in as far as they help to constitute the central allegory of the painting. *A Short Sad Book*, too, focuses on the English-French conflict, but the book firmly resists the transparency that makes West's painting effective propaganda, and it persistently turns metaphors traditionally employed to initiate such transparency – mirrors, windows, water – into metonymy. A particularly extended conversion occurs in Bowering's re-telling of Tom Thomson's death by drowning:

> ... it is not a clear lake with a body on the bottom.
> It is a body & who needs a lake.
> This is the real body of literature. (135-136)

Not even Thomson's name is fully transparent; stubbornly, the narrator misspells his name, and the index lists two Thom(p)sons.

A Short Sad Book insists on alternatives and coincidences, and it denies closure. As a whole, the book resembles Curnoe's mixed media approach and presents a series of possible openings and endings, offers a random selection of styles, and tries out various genres. Founding myths, such as the Expulsion of the Acadians and the Building of the Railway, also undergo several mutations, as their protagonists, Evangeline and John A. MacDonald, step out of the bondage of history, venture into "her/story," and engage in implausible dialogue, a "dialog" held among the trees soon to be turned into logs, then into the pages of a book. As in *Burning Water*, which was in preparation when *A Short Sad Book* appeared, Bowering translates the power relationship between his protagonists into sexual terms, but undermines MacDonald's predominance by endowing Evangeline with intellectual independence, initiative and irony, in other words, with the ability to remake history according to her own wishes. The reader is urged to measure the achievements and failures of historical figures against his own, and vice versa:

> Shove over, I want to talk to the reader. I want to say something to the reader reading. Reader reading, dont imagine any more that you can put on your invisibility suit & watch what they are doing.... Either admit that what I report of the matter is the truth of the matter or face the truth, that if you can see them they can see you. (174)

3. Jack Chambers and Autobiology

If Curnoe's work provided a model for Bowering's engagement in the making of official Canadian culture, then another London artist explored the private in ways which appealed to Bowering's own growing concern with life-writing. Seth Feldman, writing about Chambers' film *The Hart of London*, called the artist "one of the most sophisticated theorists of realism in his documentary-oriented nation" (54) and the film "in a typically Canadian fashion, a chronicle that documents the reconciliation of one man and one place over time" (55). Feldman fails to point out, however, that Chambers' procedure questions the very bases of the documentary – time, space, and perspective.

Jack Chambers settled in London, Ontario in the early sixties, after graduating from the Spanish Royal Academy of Art and spending several years in a Castilian village. In 1969, he was diagnosed as suffering from leukemia. The luminous quality of his painting *401 Towards London No 1* (1968-1969) and the famous *Sunday Morning No. 2* (1969-70), in which his two young sons watch television on a sunny winter morning, was widely perceived to be a visionary response to the impending end. But even before 1969, his work was obsessed with death, and after the artist's death nine years later, Bruce Elder concluded that "Chambers' being a youthful victim of leukemia seems one of those unhappy instances in which an artist comes to live out a fate foreshadowed in his art" (Elder 1981a: 16). Yet, a few months after being told that he had only a few months to live (in fact, he died nine years later), Chambers published his manifesto "Perceptual Realism," a powerfully life-affirming analysis of his art. The artist's role is described in terms of growth, regeneration and communion with the universe: "Art is a lower-case word; it's a craft of the natural like fruit growing on trees is a craft of nature. Man as art is the image of his nature just as mankind is the fruit of the primary process animating the earth and all in which the earth as a fruit is rooted" (Chambers 1969: 7). If the theme of death did not suddenly emerge in Chambers' work in 1969, neither did that of regeneration. In fact, the two are usually inseparably linked, as in the film *Hybrid* (1967), in which photographs of injured Vietnamese children are superimposed "on shots of flowers opening" (Lord 26), in the juxtaposition of age and youth in *Olga Visiting Mrs. V* (1964) and of tombstones and vegetation in *Olga Visiting Graham* (1964), or in the stylized still-lifes of daffodils and tulips. The cover of Bowering's *Particular Accidents: Selected Poems* (1980) bears a reproduction of Chambers' *Grass Box No. 2* (1968-70), a work in pearly-grey graphite on paper and plexiglas with purple insets. The picture is based on a photograph of Chambers mowing his lawn, but because that part of the picture had been accidentally destroyed by 1980, the Talonbooks cover leaves off the gigantic flowers intruding into the picture from the left, seemingly bent on cancelling out the lawnmower's activity. Bowering was particularly attracted to the painting, because one of his earliest stories was an absurdist parable involving a lawnmower (*Protective Footwear*).

A year after the appearance of "Perceptual Realism," Bowering wrote *Autobiology*. The book was also born out of a personal crisis, if not as acute as Chambers', and it marks a major creative shift in Bowering's career, as well as a change in his personal life. Bowering's daughter Thea was born in 1972; a photograph of father and daughter appears on the back cover, complementing a picture of a three or four-year-old Bowering with his mother on the front. If the many canvases Chambers painted of his sons during his last years courageously counterpoint his own decline, so too, although in a less poignant sense, do the children's pictures enclosing *Autobiology:* "I discovered the working was a wearing away. In the orchard at Naramata I removed my baseball cap every time & every time it was a nest of hair & I was fifteen there. The working was a wearing away" (Bowering 1972a: 43). In a conventional autobiography, the narrator separates himself clearly, if nostalgically, from his younger self, of which his own child may be a welcome or painful reflection. *Autobiology,* however, introduces a complex superimposition of times, refusing to adopt a sequential ordering of time: "the smelter is a dead fire with a dead chimney the highest structure in the area a spire I lookt up when I was five & when I was twenty & when I was thirty when I had raspberries in my back yard" (17). As well as collapsing various stages in his life in the one activity of looking up "a spire," the passage fails to separate between an adult's and a child's voice. Instead, Bowering's prose insistently repeats and varies key phrases. These repetitions blur temporal and spatial distinctions between individual sentences, which are looped together with the melodious playfulness of the *terza rima,* as in the opening "When I was thirty I had free raspberries in the backyard & I loved them. In the back yard & I ate them. & I ate them in the kitchen out of an aluminium pot. When I was thirty I loved raspberries, I loved to eat them" (7). Bowering's procedure resembles Chambers', who, in several canvases, involves the viewer in a complex layering of time. The graphite drawings he produced between 1967 and 1968, *Grass Box No. 2* among them, were mounted "in plexiglass and sealed liquid plastic and, sometimes, painted over the surface of the plastic with oil" (Elder 1981b: 65). Because the plexiglass reflects the viewer's image, he was confronted with his own presence superimposed on the multiple levels of the painting. In other words, Chambers effectively relativized the concepts of time and space, thus allowing "the dissolution of the limited self and the discovery of the grander self that encompasses the Other" (Elder 1981b: 63).

The timelessness in both men's work reinforces a pastoral element, which is, however, not unquestioningly idyllic. Ross Woodman has traced gardens which "[are] at once the garden of Eden and a graveyard where innocence is both celebrated and corrupted" throughout Chambers' work, as, for example, in his films *The Hart of London* (1968-70), *Mosaic* (1966), *Hybrid* (1967), *R34* (1967), and, particularly, in *Circle* (1968-69). Most of this film is composed of 365 shots of Chambers' own backyard filmed for "'a couple of seconds' from the same spot for a year" (Woodman 1980: 17). The effect is both peaceful and chilling, as an ordinary space with clothes-line and toys becomes monumental by virtue of its prolonged presence on the screen. Chambers' most uninhibited childhood reminiscences and celebration of the pastoral appear in his notebooks; these were included in a volume which was supervised by the artist, but not published until after his death. The lushness of the description here corresponds to the otherworldly light in *Sunday Morning No. 2* and *401 Towards London No. 1*:

> In summer our garden was rich and beautiful. Grandad was the gardener. He grew huge peonies. I buried my nose in them for the aroma and always came out sneezing. Black, red and white currants grew behind the peonies and I used to crawl around the currant bushes and pretend wonderful things ... [There were] raspberries, many flowers and an arbour of purple grapes. I remember my grandfather leaning on his shovel and smoking his pipe. (quoted in Poole n.p.)

Its experimental language notwithstanding, *Autobiology* opens on a similarly Edenic vision of a three-year-old among the raspberry bushes, a scene developed and varied throughout the book. In "Chapter 18: The Trees," the now grown-up narrator "pickt in the orchard removing cherries ... moved in the orchard thinning apples" (41) and "stood on the highest branches in the orchard & worried about the flight of [his] soul" (42). An elaboration on the tree as image of the self in Bowering's early poems, these trees, too, are an adult's extension of the child's early and intimate communion with the earth and the spiritual. But more emphatically than in the early lyrics, these trees are planted in a garden encircled and often invaded by death: "That house we lived in in Greenwood had a verandah wrapt in screen wire & a yard wrapt in white pickets taken from the old graveyard ..." (17). In both Bowering and Chambers, the circle is an ambiguous image, denoting perpetual regeneration as well as perpetual decay: appropriately, *Autobiology* opens with a description of raspberries which "always lookt so good with all their round pieces in a cone or bunch." "But," so the narrator continues, "there is a hole inside the raspberry & it could always have a bug in it" (8).

This ambiguous communion between "universal and particular" is repeated in the interchange of theme and structure in *Autobiology*, each consistently presenting a metonymic reflection of the other. The book is reproduced in typescript, underlining its character as diary kept "London, June 12, 1970–Vancouver, June 12, 1971." At the same time, the worn ribbon and the uneven margins foreground the script as physical fact more obviously than a meticulously printed manuscript would. The letters are an obstacle to be overcome, a code to be broken or discovered: "To be there but we are here, on this side of the page begging to be seen breaking" (39). Throughout the book, the breaking of the code corresponds to physical injuries and the resulting scars, as the narrator's body discovers the laws of the Kosmos: "I broke my nose on a girl's heel, I broke my foot under a ladder. I broke my nose on a baseball. I broke my finger under a wagon ... Investigate him. Seek the vestiges of his movement. Look for footprints" (45). Skin, teeth, and bones become the equivalents of the margins and edges in Bowering's earlier work. The encounter between inside and out is, however, not always as violent as the innumerable accidents and pains described in *Autobiology* seem to suggest. Occasionally, the narrator experiences "the private delight taking a part in erosion" (51) when nature proceeds in its growth and decay without external interference: "It didnt happen because I was there. I was where it happened & it happened & I knew someone must know but I wondered" (52). A similar gentleness informs the erotic passages in *Autobiology* which present a variation on the paradoxic interchangeability of inside and out in the lyrics "To Cleave" and "Inside the Tulip."

For Chambers, too, the surface of the picture is more than a seam between artifact and reality, but reproduces "the outward look which steps toward nature to find the door to beyond" (Chambers 1972: 29). Although he frequently worked from photographs, the surface of his paintings is often as elaborate as a Renaissance wall-relief, representing an intimate and complex interplay between perceiver and perceived: "Contrary to tradition, which usually moves from white paper to dark-shadowed *chiaroscuro*, he works in two directions at once: overlaying shadows with additional layers of graphite, or cutting in highlights with an eraser" (Amaya 119). In his film *The Hart of London,* which narrates the appearance and killing of a stray deer in his hometown, Chambers thematizes the ambiguity and density of this surface by projecting it onto an animal's eye: the hunted deer becomes a Rilkean beast which "lifts his eyes and looks us calmly through and through" (Woodman 1980: 62). This scene has several remarkably similar equivalents in *Autobiology,* where the narrator's "I's were watching the slow door close on the kitten" (29) and the "deer hung by his feet & his blood was red between the hairs on his side" (65).

In insisting on "this primary pattern that swings back and forth through man and nature and is the sense of all the moving parts of a moving whole" (Chambers 1969: 7), both Chambers and Bowering reject the symbol as an inappropriate verbal expression of man's control over his environment. In particular, *Autobiology* inveighs against the vocabulary of Jungian psychology and against surrealism, and it asserts, with Gertrude Stein, that "Consciousness is how it is composed" and "It is composed & not by us because we are in the composition" (33). In both men's work, the photograph, shedding the aggression associated with it in other contexts, becomes a token of humility and an assertion of life: the conventionally

Bowering and the London Scene 69

posed portrait on the cover of *Autobiology* is animated and blurred by the child's moving hand. The photograph helps to avoid "lyricism, subjective selectivity and emotional impurities that haphazardly deform and exaggerate objective reality" (Chambers 1969: 13). Chambers worked up large canvases such as *401 Towards London No. 1* and *Sunday Morning No. 2* from 8 x 10 or 16 x 20 colour photographs taken with a semi-wide-angle Contarex camera by first studying the photos for proportional and tonal qualities and for any information that the eye alone might have missed. The photographs were then transferred square by square onto the canvas, and the artist's work concentrated on increasingly minute divisions until "the description has been intentionally analyzed and integrated with the experience" (Chambers quoted in Magidson 20). Photograph and painting combined represent the artist's homage to the initial object, his attempt "to give back to objects what they initially gave to him" (Magidson 21). Because the viewer may attempt to project the "lyricism, subjective selectivity and emotional impurities," which the artist attempted to eliminate, back into the image, some of Chambers' paintings introduce structural and tonal distortion into the original photographs, so that the viewer is urged to explore each aspect of the painting separately. In *Olga and Mary Visiting* (1964-65), for instance, Olga's hand holding the tea-cup is separated from the body and suspended in mid-air; even more radical distortions appear in *Antonio and Miguel in the U.S.A.* (1965). The figures in these paintings resemble cutout shapes, and the colours suggest the matte and shiny surfaces of a photographic negative (Shadbolt 61).

In *Autobiology,* the photograph of mother and son on the cover is followed by an outline of the picture on the title-page. This is both an abstraction of the potentially sentimental photograph and an elaborate enactment of the entry into the "composition" and the "code" with which the book is concerned. However, Bowering's insistence on the significance of each moment becomes most obvious in passages where parataxis breaks the activity described into a series of discrete "stills," in which the "I" is, once again, participant in and recipient, not controller, of the scene: "I stood on the ladder plucking. I sat on the boxes smoking. I lay on the grass eating sandwiches. I walkt home from the orchard with its dust on my boots & green or red stains on my fingers" (42). *Autobiology* also mentions photographs *per se,* such as the picture of a lover ("I took her photograph & was careful with the f-stop, aiming the camera to catch the present forever") (20) or the portrait of Aunt Dorothy who "workt against TB & she died & I never saw her photograph after I passt the age when she died & I had my chest photographt to see whether I had TB" (23). In each case, the photograph remains part of the Heraklitian fluidity of time characteristic of *Autobiology* as a whole: "The baby acts before he knows about real, before he steps into the river that is a thing during an event, acted upon" (74).

Bowering and Chambers chronicle the ordinary events of their lives, but they refuse to conform to the conventions traditional autobiography would have imposed on them. Both assert that they have been "born many times in different places" or "underwent a series of births"; as true chroniclers, not historians, they remain immersed in the flow of things: "Man is not except as he does" (1972a: 74).

CHAPTER FIVE

Montreal, Guido Molinari and the *Kerrisdale Elegies*

We moved to Montreal during the middle of 1967 Expo, and while we lived there we saw the bombs, the burning university, the baseball team with the funny hats, the invasion by Canadian troops; and when the permanent nitrous fog moved below the twentieth-floor windows of the Place Ville Marie we promised ourselves and then we left for the West Coast. I put my jeans and laced boots back on and looked at my friends' faces again, a decade older, and now I was a Canadian at last. ("Montreal," *Craft Slices*)

After his year in London, Bowering arrived in Montreal just in time for Expo '67, and he stayed long enough to witness the political turmoil surrounding the sit-in at the computer centre of Sir George Williams University in 1969 (described in his poem "Sir George Computer University," *Seventy-One Poems for People*) and the October Crisis of 1970. He also, once again, encountered an art scene at a crucial point in its development, although it did not provide him with the kind of community he had found in Vancouver and, to a certain extent, in London. Roy Kiyooka was on staff at Sir George Williams University when Bowering arrived, as was Guido Molinari. Molinari's work had first been presented in Vancouver in 1964, a year before Kiyooka moved to Montreal; major shows featuring Borduas, Riopelle and Lemieux had been mounted in previous years, and the new art of Québec was as much a novelty in the west as the work of American and European painters. Kiyooka integrated himself so well into the style of the Montreal Neo-Plasticiens that he participated in a group show entitled "Seven Montreal Painters: A Lyric Plasticism" at the MIT Hayden Gallery and the Washington Gallery of Modern Art, together with Molinari, Claude Tousignant, Marcel Barbeau, Denis Juneau, and Jean Goguen.

Kiyooka's affinity to Barnett Newman antagonized the artistic establishment in Vancouver; in Montreal, Hard Edge also became the focus of nationalist/ internationalist debate, although it was here rooted in Québec's specific cultural situation. With Expo '67, important exhibitions of international art were brought to Montreal, but while these provided stimulating exposure to contemporary painting and sculpture, they were also discouraging to the local art scene whose claims to originality were being questioned by comparison: numerous art galleries closed following Expo and the number of exhibitions decreased (Robert 134f). But this potentially crippling situation became a fruitful one when it sparked discussions on originality and "différance," always sensitive issues in a postcolonial context. A particularly heated debate erupted, suitably, in 1970, when art historian François Gagnon described the work of the Neo-Plasticiens as imitative of American Hard Edge and drew specific chronological comparisons between individual Québécois and U.S. painters. Gagnon argued that the parallels were due, and probably inescapably so, to the exigences of urban space, because "notre culture urbaine [tend] vers l'espace le moins référentiel possible. Nos techniques nous permettent d'expérimenter des sensations spatiales peu communes où impressions de distance, gravitation et latéralité sont abolies" (Gagnon 1971: 47f). Gagnon's objections to the Neo-Plasticiens' work were not so much then that it did parallel that of the Americans, but that they insisted on differences which, he felt, were at best ephemeral. Responses came from Molinari and Tousignant who challenged Gagnon in a debate organized by *La Presse* (Thériault n.p.) and in written statements later published together with Gagnon's lecture and a historical overview by André Jasmin to form one of the most important theoretical documents of contemporary Québec art history (*Conférences*). Tousignant denounced Gagnon's assumptions as an act of national betrayal. In so doing, he echoed Fernand Leduc's response to Borduas when the latter, who was now working out of New York, criticized "Espace 55," a group showing in Montreal, as "behind the times" (Burnet 12). Molinari challenged Gagnon's theoretical basis step by step, pointing out to him that it was his definition of artistic development as naturally proceeding by imitation or "mimétisme" that was to be faulted for Québec's reputation as cultural backwater, not the Neo-Plasticiens's activities. In particular, Molinari took issue with Gagnon's refusal to define painterly symbolism in structuralist terms, for

Croire que les symboles (ou les images) en tant que tels constituent des mécanismes d'échange ou de communication, indépendamment de la structure et du code qui leur donnent un sens, c'est d'être aliéné à l'intérieur des mots et des gestes, des étiquettes et des signes. (Molinari 1971: 62)

Molinari further insisted that Gagnon had simplified Piaget (one of Molinari's favourite thinkers) in postulating the primacy of imitation over

Montreal, Guido Molinari and the *Kerrisdale Elegies* 73

creativity, that Gagnon had declared ephemeral a question of central ethical significance, and that he was mistaken in tracing a dependency of Québec to New York, for there was ample chronological and critical evidence to prove the reverse. Possibly as a result of this exchange, Gagnon appears to have changed his mind, for on the occasion of Molinari's 1975 retrospective he allowed that

> Far from demonstrating the 'catch-up' mentality which characterized Québec art during the 40s, Molinari's outlook denotes the end of this attitude and indicated the desire to escape from the Surrealist bracket in order to join the mainstream of contemporary abstract painting, bringing to it a new and original contribution. (Gagnon 1976: 55)

The combination of passionate militancy and considered thought in his argument confirmed once again Molinari's position as avant-gardist *par excellence*, who even as a highschool student acquired a reputation as a "peintre de fou." Clad in a dandyish redingote, he was known to recite his poems from a baby's high-chair, and the surrealist poet Claude Gauvreau enthusiastically celebrated the eccentric young painter in a now famous acclamation:

> Que veut Molinari? Molinari est-il fou? Non. Tout simplement: Guido (ou Guidon) est un prophète magnanime de la liberté. Il veut et désire – comme tous les artistes authentiques de notre pays – que la province de Québec ne soit plus une caricature de monastère spartiate. Il veut et désire que tous les cerveaux inventifs, chez nous, puissent oeuvrer dans un climat chaleureux et réceptif. (quoted in Théberge 1976: 10)

Gauvreau's salute is permeated by the ecstatic language of surrealism, but from the beginning of his career, Molinari defined himself as working on the edge of every single movement he has been associated with, and he once addressed a telegram to a Montreal paper, complaining that it had called him an "automatist" and claiming to be "le théoricien du molinarisme" instead (Molinari: 1976:14). Inspired by surrealist experiments in automatic writing, he radicalised their procedure by producing a series of drawings and poems in the dark. This, he felt, would abolish the last vestiges of the illusionist space to which the surrealists, despite the "oneirisme" of their works, had remained indebted. The elimination of figure-ground compositions central to illusionist space (a development he perceived as beginning with Cézanne and progressing through the work of the Cubists, Mondrian and Pollock), remained one of Molinari's main concerns as "une dimension éthique et humaniste essentielle, où culmine l'efficacité sociale, psychologique et esthétique de l'*oeuvre* d'art abstraite" (Molinari 1971: 65).

Molinari's critique of surrealism may serve as an entry-point to a comparison with Bowering's esthetic, for Bowering too has both participated in and rejected this movement. Several of his works associated with the Montreal period were, in ostentatious contrast to the crafted imagist poems of earlier years, written by dictation. In "Stab" (*In the Flesh*), he asserts:

> When I feel like it
> I will stop writing & it will be enough –
> Any other kind of poem is a lie

The same kind of determination to yield to a given form instead of shaping it, permeates *Genève* (1971), a book responding to the thirty-eight cards of the Geneva tarot deck, but rigorously eliminating any references to the history and symbolism of the games:

(I make no assumptions
about their meanings,
                   they
are such strangers to me; seeing them,
I will tell what they look like,

not in circles
but over their hill, me
the horizon.)

In practising writing "by dictation," Bowering was, however, not interested in reaching the subconscious, an entity which, he argues, does not exist at all: *Genève* was published a year after *Autobiology*, where Stein's "consciousness is how it is composed" is a recurrent key-phrase. In contrast to Freudian psychology, which separates the psyche into often antagonistically opposed rational and irrational levels and, in so doing, places the origin of the subject-object division within man himself, Bowering and Molinari accept no such borderline.

Although both experience, within themselves, the continuing tyranny of inbred dualistic perceptions of reality, their understanding of form does not allow for a division between cerebrally controlled structure and emotionally generated chaos. In his blindfolded drawings, Molinari discovered a re-current composition of space which then also informed canvases created under studio conditions: "a more static left side, a rather vertical

Montreal, Guido Molinari and the *Kerrisdale Elegies* 75

movement at left, then a movement towards the right top corner, with a counterbalance mass towards the bottom right corner" (Molinari quoted in Walsh 3f). Bowering too observed unplanned constancies in his composition and used spatial metaphors to describe the resulting "configurations":

> The falling bricks
> catch that light
>   & scatter it
> into new configurations
>
>   half random, but toucht
>   with art
>   (*Genève*)

The most complex parallels between Bowering and Molinari's art may be drawn in an area where Bowering understands his own life as a configuration "half random, but toucht / with art." *Autobiology* was one such text; another is the elegy, a genre which has held a central place in Bowering's work almost from the beginning. Usually defined as a lament for the death of a beloved person, the elegy in Bowering's *oeuvre* has over the years become a lament for the dead and the living, culminating in *Kerrisdale Elegies* as his most ambitious and justly acclaimed masterpiece. The Montreal years represent an important phase in Bowering's work on the elegy, for the end of the seventies saw the death of several members of the Beat generation, whose infatuation with their own youth and attractiveness made physical decay doubly unbearable. In 1970, Ann Charters compiled *Scenes along the Road: Photographs of the Desolation Angels 1944-1960*, a volume including Allen Ginsberg's elegiac poems "Neal's Ashes," "Memory Gardens," and "In a Car." Bowering paid homage to Neal Cassady ("what a driver") in *Allophanes* (1976), and to Kerouac in Chapter 13 of *Autobiology*, but more significantly, he began to record his own decay in obsessive detail. *In the Flesh* (1973), a volume of poetry which first proposed the severe division of his *oeuvre* (and life) into successive creative decades as if this order were a scaffolding keeping a disintegrating existence in place, contains no fewer that ten elegiac poems. Besides works dedicated to Bowering's father, Red Lane and Sam Perry, there are pieces such as the following, which are in sharp contrast with "the private delight taking a part in erosion" celebrated in *Autobiology*:

> We lost parts of us,
> whiskers hair fingernails pieces

of dead skin
>cut off, scraped away.
("Barber Chair")

& I am composed
of particles forever leaving
my organism, hair, nails
>("Midnight Lunch")

Feel pieces of teeth break inward,
useless mineral in the mouth,
minutes of death to chew over
& spit into the hand.
>("Motel Age Thoughts")

Published a decade after *In the Flesh*, *Kerrisdale Elegies* absorbs these self-pitying lyrics into a poem of grand design, Bowering's "definitive book of poetry" (Bowering 1988d: 68). Here, his favourite metaphor of the poet as tree, "a branch, a singing bird will stand on for a moment," becomes nothing less than a modern version of the medieval tree of life, often depicted as sprouting from the cross of suffering and death. (It is an appropriate coincidence that Kiyooka should focus on a similar vision in *The Pear Tree Pomes*, published only a few years after *Kerrisdale Elegies*.) The tree of life/cross of suffering is the most central of a series of oxymora in *Kerrisdale Elegies*, and many of these oxymora also have affinities to medieval mysticism: the "rose-petal [that] exudes poison in bright sunlight," the "toasted flakes on my cherry tree," the wheel that captures "bright circles of colour" but also descends to the chambers of the dead, the shroud which a young child carries "with him on the first day of school." Medieval is also the idea of man's place in a Great Chain of Being, his existence staked out by the lowly animals at his feet, "a muscular dog," "these curled insects that live under the tatters of my gladiola," and by the "exalted" ones above his head, "a flock of noisy starlings [that] leaps into the sky." Yet earth and sky are linked in a cycle which may reverse their positions:

>Every back yard is prowled by cats
with eyes of sharp grief,
>>fixed on birds
that fill the trees and rooftops with songs of their agony.

In most of the poems of his "post-lyrical" phase, Bowering conscientiously destroys any incipient lyricism as an unacceptable expression of self-indulgence: "I will always want to open a veil before beauty one day / & next day melt it down with coarse salt," he says in *Allophanes*. Despite occasional interjections such as "Oh oh, says the anxious reviewer, / this poet is not in control of his materials" or the self-conscious comment "That / I should say such a word in a poem," the language of *Kerrisdale Elegies* is "much more lush and ornate ... than Bowering would usually write" (Bowering 1988d: 88). The ironies and tensions the poem does introduce are conveyed so subtly that the stately decorum of the poem is never fully unbalanced.

In previous poems by Bowering using the tree metaphor, "Metaphor 1" in particular, word and visual design are interlaced and played off against each other. In *Kerrisdale Elegies,* this interaction becomes a central concern, because in addition to exploring the tension between image and word, the work is also written "against Rilke" (Bowering 1988d: 68) and the German poet's specific aesthetic vision. Rilke, who had acquired a considerable following among English and American poets over the years, came under close scrutiny in the years following the 1975 centenary of his birth; few commentators uncritically endorsed his enchantment with aestheticism and aristocracy, or his aversion to technology; some even suggested that his elitism carried fascist elements. [1] Bowering, who is both attracted and repulsed by the *Duino Elegies* and what they stood for, had to make his ambiguous response to Rilke literally visible:

I first wrote [the *Kerrisdale Elegies*] in long lines like Rilke's, and the rhythm was all wrong: it was sounding too much like a translation. So I just re-wrote it with a different page. Originally I wrote them in exam booklets – long, long lines written really small. But now I've got all the white space caused by editing it. Part of my sense too was a writing against Rilke, you know. I use a lot of slang and low culture which he would never do, would never condone. (Bowering 1988d: 68)

Kerrisdale Elegies may then be described as a sculptured or sculptural poem, whose interaction with the time and space surrounding it is a large-scale expression of the poet's esthetic creed. [2] It is also a critique of earlier concepts, specifically Rilke's but also Bowering's own, for the *Elegies* contain parodic echoes of many of his earlier poems. In this insistence on the ethical component of space, Bowering's concerns coincide with Molinari's, whose theoretical statements on his art indicate that he subjects it to similarly fundamental considerations. Both Bowering and Molinari have chosen large formats to give "room" to space. *Kerrisdale Elegies* is a poem of almost 150 pages, while Molinari's *Quantificateur* series (first shown in 1979) contains paintings measuring a width of twenty-one feet; others are close to ten feet high. Not even this vastness, however, is enough to accommodate the energy the paintings and poems contain. Several lines in the *Elegies* extend beyond the frame of the page and have to be bridled by brackets, as in "Elegy Four":

They fell into shapes on the floor,
                           constellations
observed in Cathay and Tical.
                           Voices murmured around
                                       [them.
They would disappear when I learned
to buy my own books.
I was in no hurry to grow,
                or so I thought,
                        but I moved
                        [to where the stars
were fewer,

In Molinari's large canvases, stripes and colours often establish a mnemonic sequence which extends beyond the picture frame, the more so since the colours may have been juxtaposed to create a pulsating effect which radiates beyond the canvas itself:

Le tableau de grand format pose le spectateur dans un environnement où il sera d'avantage concerné, non seulement par la structure sémantique du tableau, mais par une expérimentation physique des différents phénomènes énergétiques qui constituent le champ opératoire qu'est l'oeuvre. (Molinari 1976: 66)

The square page of the *Elegies* serves as a field upon which the tree of life is erected. It is, by necessity, flattened onto the page, but the poem consistently evokes a space of cosmic extensions, in which all components are in such constant dynamic communion that it is virtually impossible to find short quotations to illustrate the point:

Out there was the fortunate fall, mountains
glistening with creation,
                       a glacier between them,
flowing bright out of the working god's fingers,
first orchards rising from the melt, light
shaped on crest and cut,
                          the roll of storms
shaking new, flattening the grass,
                              quick lakes
a scatter of mirror, clouds in them, all
favour, all breaking side to side, all

being outside,
        all blossom.
    ("Elegy 2")

Here, Bowering couples the participle of the present, whose particular combination of stasis and momentum he has explored in many previous poems, with a breath pattern which captures the poet's awe before creation and his total immersion in it. Especially effective is the repetition of "all" followed by an enjambment, as well as the last line "all blossom," each of which requires a deep intake of breath followed by a long exhalation.

Bowering's exploration of a "dancing" space has a remarkable equivalent in Molinari's 1987 work *Dance Soupir*, in which four very large canvasses entirely in red form a concave wall engulfing the viewer and "radiat[ing] colour while it absorbs the natural light streaming through the huge windows of the studio" ("Simply Red": 15). The title links painter, work and viewer in an inseparable, almost physiological, entity that evokes the shelter of the womb. That shelter, and the young child's self-sufficient creativity is as central to *Kerrisdale Elegies* as it is to Molinari's esthetics, which openly declare their indebtedness to child psychologist Jean Piaget's studies *La Représentation de l'espace chez l'enfant* (1948) and *La Construction du réel* (1950). This connection has been explored in some detail by Molinari's wife, the art historian Fernande St. Martin, in *Structures de l'espace pictural* (1968) and *Les Fondements topologiques de la peinture: essai sur les modes de représentation de l'espace, à l'origine de l'art enfantin et de l'art abstrait* (1980). Of particular interest to St. Martin and Molinari were the alternatives which children's art offered to "Euclidean" space with its insistence on figure-ground construction. In contrast to the latter which postulates one single perspective, children's art introduces multiple points of view and, in the early stages, all but ignores the notion of emptiness which make the figure-ground construction possible. Instead, a child's drawing may be populated by designs densely structuring the *surface* in rhythms of similarity and contrast. In his black-and-white paintings (1951-1961), Molinari experiments with the two non-colours black and white, shades of which have traditionally created the *chiaroscuro* and the illusion of a recession of space. Molinari first separated white and black in Hard Edge juxtapositions to give each equal presence on the surface of the canvas. In order to dispel any similarities with a predictable, if open, grid-system, he further introduced kinetic designs creating a "purely 'polysemic' space" (Campbell 1989: 24).

At the centre of the *Kerrisdale Elegies*, there is a child, "new for his Kerrisdale mom," who seems to generate from within the poem the "interactionist" space Piaget observed in children's art, where intuition and intelligence are inseparably fused. Throughout the *Elegies*, the lines are opened up by large white spaces which, together with the black print, form energy vectors crossing, and transcending, the page. In the section "He was new for his Kerrisdale mom," the lines tidily alternate between the right and the left, as the reader's eyes follow a series of declarative sentences chronicling the child's progress according to the "unitarist" vision of the adult:

He was new for his Kerrisdale mom,
                                he grew
like a poppy in her garden.
                                She kept him in after dark,
safe from midnight vapours.
                                He was her
riddle of bones.
                        She was his tidy doorway,
keeping him safe,
                            showing him his new world
a little at a time.
                            She gave him a wooden gun
when he was eight.
                            She read him stories
in which children win
                              but grow up anyway.

Subsequent sections of "Elegy 3," however, describe the child's dreams and games, activities in which the bridge between reason and inspiration is collapsed. The personal pronouns "he" and "she" blend into "you" and "he," then into "I," as the speaker of the poem yields his place to the child:

What am I doing in the kitchen?

I'd rather be upstairs with my toys.
                                I know
how they work.

In "Lying in the dark," the linear sequence of "He was new for his Kerrisdale mom" opens into a far more complex syntactic and visual pattern, in which the verse resembles building blocks from which the child constructs his world. The white spaces on these pages do not signify the void, but a space with infinite possibilities, and the viewer's glance is not bridled into a left-right motion only, but tries to encompass all of the trajectories emanating from the "passive vacancy" of the sleeping child:

>   he sleeps,
> but he dreams too;
>   and where he now soars
> there are no mothers,
>   there are only
> stellar monsters to be loved,
>   there are galaxies
> of fire just missing the cockpit.
>   He is inside,
> where you have been but can never enter.

The poem further develops a polysemic space by interrupting the poem with unidentified quotations from French and Québec poetry (see Kamboureli 1987), first establishing a mnemonic sequence by placing these quotations at the end of a poem, then destroying this sequence by placing them within the poem or by leaving quotations out altogether in some poems. This is only the most radical of several similar strategies in the *Elegies*, where certain key-phrases such as "Being dead is no bed of roses" reappear in variations as "Still, being dead / is no bed of roses" and "It is no bed of roses, / being dead." The recurrence of this phrase is not grounded in any discernible poetic "laws," for the poet refuses to comply with the exigencies of the "closing couplet." The *Elegies* endorse asymmetry then, as do paintings by Molinari, such as *Untitled* (1958) where "the unequal number of colour bands, their asymmetrical placement, their varying length and the off-centre focal point elude [mnemonic] grouping" (Szylinger 1982: n.p.).

In his paintings Molinari gives equal intensity to each colour by using the spatula, spray, or roller. There is no hierarchy of intensity or presence among the colours, an effect Molinari further emphasized by abandoning, particularly in his work from the sixties, horizontal stripes, because he felt that the figure-ground convention by which they were informed would affect the equality of the colours. Bowering translates a similar principle into various visual and linguistic procedures. The large white spaces that break up *Kerrisdale Elegies* affect the horizontal Gutenberg line to the point where the reader is sometimes tempted to read the poem as two (or more) vertical columns interlaced with each other. Nor does the poem observe stylistic hierarchies: the recurrent key phrases mentioned earlier merge in and out of "high" and "low" diction depending on the phrases with which they are juxtaposed. A particularly complex example appears in "Elegy 2":

> She says
> I've got you under my skin, yes, she says
> You walk with me wherever I go,
> you are
> the weather.
>
> I reply with a call for help,
> I'm disappearing,
> there's a change in the weather.

Throughout, the *Elegies* insist on parataxis to underline the independence and opacity of each thing, a method which Rilke had first observed and admired in the brushstrokes of Cézanne, who boldly juxtaposed primary colours until then considered incompatible. There are flashes of primary colours in the *Elegies* as well (all the more remarkable because Bowering rarely uses colour in his work): "the green diamond at Little Mountain," "the yellow leaves," "this sound / coming out blue." But while underlining the independence of each element, parataxis paradoxically also highlights their interdependence, because the dignity of one element can only be appreciated in juxtaposition with another. On his return to Vancouver in the early seventies, Bowering acquired a number of paintings by Brian Fisher, and while their affinity to Hard Edge makes their appeal to Bowering similar to Molinari's work, they also convey the paradoxical cohabitation of independence and interdependence in a very specific way.

In his "Statement" for the 1967 Centennial exhibition at the Norman MacKenzie Art Gallery in Regina, Fisher denounced man's progressive divorce from his natural environment, and he echoes Bowering almost word by word when he proclaims, "Man now has to consider his consciousness as a co-ordinate in any given situation" (47) and "[M]an is beginning to examine the dynamic inter-relationships of things – the patterns of structure, the configurations of energy fields, the interactions of competing aggregates" (50). In Fisher's paintings, this programme is translated into an interaction of straight and curved lines. The result are pulsating moiré-patterns, molluscan equivalents of cosmic flux. In his celebrated *Indicant No. 2*, this interaction intensifies in "a circular concavity" at the centre of the canvas, an "indicant" of "an eventual curvature of space outside the painting" (Pinney 1969: 42). Fisher insists that the apparent intellectualism of his paintings has its source in "sensual immediacy" (Fisher 49), and that a curve describes both enclosure and opening of the human body. The parallels with Bowering's love poetry, "Inside the Tulip," in particular, are apparent; in *Kerrisdale Elegies*, which otherwise casts a cold eye on his early lyrics, Bowering reiterates his creed:

>   The open had been
> just beyond her,
>   but you were in her, she
> is after all,
>   the world.

   ("Elegy 8")

CHAPTER SIX

The *Burning Water* Trilogy

1. Postmodernism, Colony, Nation: The Melvillean Texts of Bowering and Beaulieu

Kerouac said ... that he sailed on the Pequod for fifteen years and never saw one single whale, just a lot of flounders. And I really respect a guy that will do that and then write about them. ("14 Plums: An Interview")

The *Burning Water* trilogy translates into epic scale the drawing which Bowering included in *Allophanes* and which depicted man in a diamond field staked out by the poles of water, earth, fire, and air. *Burning Water* (1979), the first volume, is set on water, and it speaks of the fire destroying the presumptuous maps of the explorer: burning, the paper dissolves into thin air. With *Caprice* (1987), the trilogy moves inland; and the remaining volume "will have to be in the air, right?" (Bowering 1988d: 56). Each volume deals with a different time-period – *Burning Water* takes place in 1790, *Caprice* in 1890, and the final volume is projected to be set in 1990. The trilogy may then be called a historical novel chronicling the genesis of British Columbia. At the same time, however, it is also a complex parody of historical fiction and related genres, the travelogue and the Western, and it is a deconstruction of the imperialist / racist / sexist agenda traditionally shaping these fictions. This approach has nothing to do with "wallowing in post-colonial guilt," (Scott 9), but everything with commitment to the political responsibilities of the writer. The *Burning Water* trilogy earns Bowering a place among those post-colonial authors who have successfully challenged and subverted the discourse of the ruler, including his image-making. In his critique of modernism in "The Three-Sided Room: Notes on the Limitations of Modernist Realism" and in "Modernism Could Not Last Forever" (*The Mask in Place*), Bowering consistently refers to visual forms such as the photograph, the stained-glass window, and the television screen. In his novels, he expands his critique to include visual imperialism.

The *Burning Water* Trilogy

It is no coincidence that some of the most technically daring postmodernist writing has come out of former colonies, notably from the countries of Latin America. Here, the break with realism implies a reaction not only against literary modes preferred by the mother-country, but also against its concepts of time and place, and of personal and collective identity. Realism is considered an instrument placed at the service of the conqueror to perpetuate the reflection of his world image as the only one possible. In other words, the colony is expected to duplicate, to emulate even, the pattern set out for it by the colonizer. Critics have widely commented on the obsessive reappearance of the mirror-image in Borges and others, but here the mirror has become the threshold to strange worlds in which the principles of chronological time, geographical space, and psychologically plausible characterization have given way to "oneirism," the logic of the dream. The fantasy in novels like *Cien años de soledad* (1967), far from being a fanciful ornament, is no less than a refusal to comply with the conqueror's attempt to impose a continuation of his own history on those he has submitted to himself.

While rejecting realism as the colonizer's mode, Latin American authors have not, however, created an altogether new literary form of expression for themselves. Strong associations between their work and the baroque have been noticed,[1] placing them in a tradition in which a seemingly revolutionary artistic development is anchored in a model far enough removed in time and nature to provide the frame of reference for a renewed and inspiring discussion of it. Some postmodernists in Québec and English Canada have found such a model in Herman Melville's work, particularly in *Moby Dick*. The reasons for his attractiveness to authors like Bowering and Victor-Lévy Beaulieu are obvious; Melville helped shape a distinctively American literary voice without falling prey to patriotic propaganda and can therefore provide useful inspiration; moreover, he has assumed the status of a "classic" and escapes – at least superficially – the reproach of being a proponent of contemporary U.S. literature, an influence feared and rejected by Canadian nationalists in English Canada and Québec alike.

It is, however, characteristic of the Canadian literary situation – as Beaulieu and Bowering understand it – that they should derive their inspiration secondhand, from a writer who, in his imitation of Renaissance narrative, contributed to formulating an unmistakably American form of fiction. Melville's achievement interjects itself between the Canadian authors and their reaction to European predominance; in both cases, this interjection is eventually perceived as a problematic one because Melville was a member of a society that became as imperialist in its aspirations as the mother-country had been and his linguistic strategies helped to entrench prejudices which the Declaration of Independence had presumably abolished (Knutson). One remedy – or attempted remedy – in correcting the negative side-effects of literary *décalage* consists in perceiving Melville as part of a utopian concept of America, the promise of a mythic new space in which European notions of man-made order are no longer applicable. Charles Olson's *Call Me Ishmael* (1947), combining poetry and scholarship in its exalted celebration of the American space on the one hand and its identification of Shakespearean influence on Melville on the other, is mentioned time and again in discussions of Melville's role in Canadian postmodernism (see, for example, Mandel); however, it is difficult to ignore the fact that Olson, too, has been one of the chief targets of Canadian criticism of so-called cultural imperialism, and that he bypassed the question of native land claims by mythologizing both Indians and Americans (Knutson). Another attempted corrective is to translate Melville's enormous vision, which, despite its fragmented encyclopedism, still pursues the absolute, into the self-ironic pursuit of "a great many particulars" (*Allophanes*) or else "just a lot of flounders."

Burning Water and *Monsieur Melville* are not only motivated by their authors' common interest in Melville but also indicate an area for genuine comparative work in the two major Canadian literatures, work otherwise often inspired by extra-literary (that is to say politically contrived) reasons. Although René Lapierre, in his review of *En Eaux troubles*, the French translation of *Burning Water*, admits that he has never heard of Bowering before, his assessment of the book is considerably more sympathetic than that found in most English reviews, and Michel Beaulieu lauded Bowering generally as a "[n]ovateur, doué d'un régistre des plus étendus ..., il est de ceux qui ont l'esprit constamment en éveil;" moreover, Beaulieu commended western writers for their efforts to decentralize Canadian literature (Beaulieu, M. 56). I suggest that at least part of the emphatically negative response *Burning Water* received in the English-Canadian press has its root in Bowering's association with TISH and the Black Mountain poets, and in the determination of nationalist critics to link postmodernist experimentation to an influx of American individualism and anarchism, when *Burning Water* in fact uses postmodernism to critique *both* of these attitudes in imperialism *per se*. Québec writers and critics, on the other hand, have consistently linked experimental writing with national self-liberation; unburdened by the *specific* associative ballast English reviewers have to contend with, Lapierre appreciates Bowering's book for its daring form. A similar (and, as yet, rather stronger) case can be made for the interest found among innovative English-Canadian translators, critics, and writers in authors such as Beaulieu, Brossard, Bersianik. Whereas I have not found any evidence that Beaulieu is aware of Bowering's work, Bowering calls Victor-Lévy Beaulieu his "brother" in *A Short Sad Book*, and in *Craft Slices*, he includes the Québec author in the "Sheila Watson canon" of writers who have "fought for a post-modernist, deconstructivist writing that discards the mock-objectivity of realism and declares for fabrication" (55).

One feature in Melville's composite story-telling seems to have especially attracted both Bowering and Beaulieu: his insistence on visual allusions. In a concept of history based on phenomenology, the senses – particularly that of vision – traditionally receive special attention as potential recipients of knowledge. In a narrative in which language, spoken as well as written, becomes increasingly suspect as the colonizer's weapon, images hold the promise of an alternative code, although they too come under scrutiny as conditioned by pre-shaped vision. It is on the variations of such Melvillean images as the oil-painting at the entrance to the Spouter-Inn, Quequeg's tattoos, the doubloon aboard the *Pequod*, the hieroglyphics on the whale's skin, Ahab's maps, and others that I wish to concentrate here.

Both Bowering and Beaulieu understand their writing as a serial effort in which one central subject matter is, as in Melville's composite fiction, approached from various generic angles, in an attempt at counteracting the simplifying linearity realist writing imposes on the concepts expressed in it. Thus, Bowering uses the figure of Captain George Vancouver both in a serial poem *George, Vancouver* (1976) and in his novel *Burning Water* (1980), while providing cross-references to others of his books, such as *Mirror on the Floor* (1967), through the autobiographical character of George Delsing, "a projection of myself more than anyone else is" (Bowering 1971 / 72: 45-47). Beaulieu, an even more prolific writer, combines his *oeuvre* in large cycles, e.g. *La vraie saga des Beauchemin* and *Voyageries* among them, in which a central theme is approximated through various personae as well as through unorthodox fictional genres such as "lamentation" for *N'évoque plus que le désenchantement de ta ténèbre, mon si pauvre Abel* (1976), "lecture-fiction" for *Monsieur Melville* (1978) and "romaman" for *Una* (1980). Even within the individual work, Beaulieu and Bowering use a "mixed language" (Berger 1975: 48), which alternates between fiction and documentary and involves visual codes other than letters, namely pictorial material such as the recurrent Chinese character in *Burning Water* and the illustrations in the *Voyageries*. "Mixed language" contributes to formulating a sense of synchronic rather than diachronic patterning; history, personal and national, is understood as a redefinable present rather than as an irrevocably interpreted past; Beaulieu's tendency to rewrite and republish some of his older novels to adapt them to his present development as a writer may serve as a particularly striking evidence of this notion. The writer's presence (or that of his persona) is strong in both Bowering's and Beaulieu's novel; he is a reader of, and commentator on, literature. Both seek to establish the honesty of their interpretation by carefully describing their own reactions, although the result may be yet another lie, a "lecture-fiction."

In *Burning Water*, Bowering presents the fictional conflict between Captain George Vancouver and his ship's surgeon Menzies, whose contrasting modes of assimilating their environment make them not only Canadian counterparts of Ahab and Ishmael, but also the polarities between which the narrator of the novel attempts to situate his own writing: on the one hand, there is George Vancouver, who, like Ahab, believes that the charting of new territory mirrors one's personal and national philosophy; on the other, there is Menzies, Ishmael's twin, who postulates that the meaning of each new territory must be patiently deciphered and efficiently catalogued. Bowering captures this dialectic in the opposition of two different kinds of image-making. The image-making typical of Vancouver is that of mapping and of the painting of historical *tableaux*; Bowering conceives of both strategies as violent and narcissistic, their physical correlatives being Vancouver's lust in beating a sailor's body into submission and his homosexual affair with Quadra, the emulated mirror-image of his own aspirations.[2] Bowering exposes maps and historical paintings as fanciful, politically opportune deformations of reality that belong to the instrumentarium of Machiavelli. At the same time, he describes these images as emblems of self-destruction; not accidentally is Vancouver described as a man of ill health and Ahab as a one-legged sailor.

In an effort at collecting empirically accurate evidence, the narrator of *Burning Water* visits museums, galleries, and archives; yet he realizes that here, too, image-making becomes self-generating and takes place in a world without exit; instead of approaching reality, the narrator finds himself caught up in the dilemma of his own characters: it is almost impossible to avoid "yet another sequence of rooms filled with artifacts" (Bowering 1980b: 192), whether they be pictorial or literary; thus, the echoes of Shakespeare's art resound in Melville's work, inspiring and crippling it at the same time. With the help of his pen and an airplane (both described as tubular shapes), the narrator of *Burning Water* tries to overcome the compulsion of linearity and influence and create a locus of actual history in his own consciousness, here, Trieste, South America, and the Pacific North-West converge with the past, the present and an imagined future and the light piercing Quadra's cabin-window is the light of the sun that "had risen high over the island's mountains, and laid generous light over everything on the sea, the way it does in the morning at Trieste" (169). In a similar strategy, Bowering strips historical *tableaux* of their characteristics as static artifacts by translating them into the dynamics of parody.

Vancouver loved to jump out of a boat, stride a few paces up the beach and announce: "I claim this new-found land for his Britannic Majesty in perpetuity, and name it New Norfolk."

Usually the officers and men stood around fairly alertly, holding flags and oars and looking about for anyone who did not agree. (26-27)

More significantly, fiction relieves its creator and its creatures from historical strictures, and Vancouver's story closes with a death mythologically more fitting than his historical end: like Narcissus and Ahab, Vancouver drowns in the sea that he tried to make the reflection of his own self.

Whereas the trappings of historical oil-painting allow the subjects depicted to slip into a mythological scene as if it were held out like a garment "for the spectator-owner to put his arms into and wear" (Berger 1972: 102), William Blake created spiritual, transparent images strange enough to disallow identification. Bowering contrasts George Vancouver's megalomaniac search for enshrinement in historical artifact with the presence, in London, of William Blake who frightened George III into the awareness of his own mortality by confronting him with the picture of Nebuchadnezzar crawling naked on his hands and feet. Revealingly, Blake's work is unacceptable to two Englishmen who discuss Pacific sea otter skin as if it were yet another protective shell for the "kingdoms of the civilized world." Their understanding of Blake's art would shatter their premise; logically, they block him out by referring to him as a "lunatic called Black, or Block, dash it, I cannot recall" (205). Colour, too, may be part of a restrictive code; Blake's insistence on pale images or garish, unrealistic colour assumes the function of the whiteness of Moby Dick's skin: the absence of a familiar and therefore soothing impression on the eye jolts the observer into an uncomfortably new, aesthetically (and morally) unsettling experience.

The second group of image-making converges in Vancouver's opposite, Ishmael's literary brother Menzies. He reads the hieroglyphics of the Pacific North-West by studying the plants of the land, its artifacts, its languages. Like Blake, he considers nature worshippers to be atheists and shocks his captain with "the utter lack of expression" (165) on his face when he shoots an albatross and, without regard to its literary connotations, examines it for "everything from diet to diseases of the talons" (87). Vancouver places his stamp on the new-found land, by inscribing his feelings "all over the long-living geography of the Southwestern half of the world" in "Port Discovery," "Port Conclusion," "Port Decision," "Cape Quietude," "Hesitation Harbour," and "The Strait of Inconsistence" (79). Menzies, by contrast, collects samples of the flora and shelters them carefully on the "Discovery," to be taken back to England. The image typical of Menzies, the "true Western Man" (108), is that of the Chinese character prefacing the different parts of *Burning Water*. It is the logo of a sailing-boat taken from the notebook in which Bowering drafted the novel; the ambiguous nature of the logo as both a sign for Vancouver's ship, and for the literary vehicle (or vessel) carrying the tenor of metaphor – derives from Menzies' understanding that charting strategies do not equal the thing, that "the language is burning" (Bayard, David 95) and must be tended like a flame. Menzies is, however, not quite like Ishmael. In his lovemaking with a native woman, he too is a potential colonizer, who only teaches her the words she needs to satisfy his lust. If she is not a victim but takes all the pleasure she can from him, it is her merit, not his; Menzies' thoughts are in England, with Mrs. Banks. By contrast, Ishmael's friendship with Quequeg is more that of equals than Melville's prejudicially freighted language appears to allow; Susan Knutson has persuasively shown how Melville's discourse frequently muffles the racial and sexual radicalism of the book, a radicalism better communicated by Ishmael's reading, in Pidgin English, of Quequeg's tattoos than by their dialogue.

Beaulieu, too, is aware of the greater richness in potential meaning found in ideograms. *N'évoque plus que le désenchantement de ta ténèbre, mon si pauvre Abel*, the volume of the *Voyageries* in which *Monsieur Melville* begins to crystallize, is illustrated with various examples of such lettering, and he mentions that his favourite edition of *Moby Dick* is the Japanese, "parce que les mots étrangers, pourtant si incompréhensibles, sont des images du merveilleux de la baleine blanche" (Beaulieu, V.-L. 1976: 174). Yet Beaulieu's fascination with ideograms has a different root from Bowering's. In the *Voyageries* (and particularly in the 500-page *Monsieur Melville*) pictures rank at least equally in power of expression to the text; they are not illustrations in the traditional sense of being subservient appendages to the words, but illustrations in Blake's sense of relaying an additional dimension of meaning. In the opening pages of *Monsieur*

Melville, Melville's photograph is described as a crutch, meant to help Abel over the threshold into the interior of Melville's oeuvre. The analogy to a passage into a *camera obscura* is not only captured in the wide black margins framing the first illustrations in the book, but also in the black pages opening and closing it within double-pages representing a boat, obviously once again a representation of the vessel of creation. Pictures appear as they would intrude upon the author's mind as he is writing; apart from numerous illustrations of whales and whaling, there are photos from Melville's and Beaulieu's family albums, pictures of various other authors such as Flaubert and Joyce, reproductions of paintings, excerpts from *Finnegans Wake,* and so on. The images may be blurred, they may appear repeatedly, they may appear in different focus. Especially in *N'évoque plus,* the shortest and most cohesive volume of the *Voyageries,* the pictures could be grouped together into different interwoven strands of leitmotifs, to suggest the writer's simultaneous engagement in past, present, and future projects and his commitment to artists who preceded his own effort. Beaulieu underlines the presence of a web of intertextualities in various ways: he prefaces *N'évoque plus* with the drawing of a maze, uses pages in different shades to suggest concurrent thoughts, and develops an elaborate system of parentheses.

It should be obvious from the above that the pictures in the *Voyageries* are to be understood almost as projections of the narrator's brain; they lose the identity they may have had in their original context and become thoroughly coloured with the personality of whoever happens to be the narrator, a process especially well illustrated in the 1979 edition of Beaulieu's *Les Grands-pères,* where the meanderings of grand-père's thoughts are contained within a cover bearing the photographs of the back of the head of Beaulieu's own grandfather. Pictures are only weak reflections of the mind's images, but they are preferable to writing alone because "Écriture ne constitue pas une orientation parce que cela ni commence ni s'achève, parce que cela ne fait que se recommencer pour occuper tout le champ de ses fissures et, par cela même, en produire de nouvelles, et d'autres encore jusqu'à l'extinction de soi" (Beaulieu, V.-L. 1978: 14). Illustrations, in Beaulieu, are expression of the writer's anxiety vis-à-vis the irremediable inadequacy of language, of a longing for perfect mimesis, a concern which Bowering, for his part, seems to have dismissed as irrelevant and anachronistic.

Whereas *Burning Water* re-enacts the conflict of Ahab and Ishmael in Vancouver and Menzies, externalizing the narrator as the third participant of the confrontation, *Monsieur Melville* internalizes that conflict and places it exclusively within the fictionalized reader of Melville's work, a reader schizophrenically torn between the pursuit of the absolute code (Ahab) and a recording of the fragmented, unsatisfactory evidence about it (Ishmael). Abel Beauchemin, the narrator of *Monsieur Melville*, perceives in Herman Melville a mirror of his own anguish, but also the proof that ingenious writing is possible in spite or even as a result of it. Reading voraciously everything written by and about Melville will, Beauchemin hopes, leave him "un moi-même différent de ce que je suis" (1: 24). His "lecture-fiction" resembles in many ways the reverential glossing and paraphrasing typical of medieval exegesis; Abel seems like a monk who perceives the magic of truth in the very lettering of Melville's writing. Rigorous intellectual analysis would destroy that magic and assimilate Melville to Beauchemin's mind, instead of allowing Abel to model himself carefully after Melville. Thus, Abel criticizes Jean Giono's *Pour saluer Melville* for making of the American author "rien de moins qu'un autre Giono". (3: 13) Understandably, Beauchemin fears to lose his purpose among the discouragingly extensive detail he has collected, and he attempts to exorcise this fear by asserting once again his fetishist belief in the power of images: each page of the *Voyageries* bears in the upper right hand corner the small logo of a whale, an image possibly inspired by the description of a whaling log in Melville's *Mardi,* in which a successful hunt is signalled by filling up, in jet black, the outline figure of the animal.

Although everything in *Monsieur Melville* points toward an almost naive faith in the power of images, Abel Beauchemin's self-description is not static and certainly not to be equated with Beaulieu's self-understanding as a writer. Among the pictures illustrating *N'évoque plus* are the illustrations of Lewis Carroll's *Alice in Wonderland,* Hans Baldung Grien's *The Three Ages of Woman and Death,* Manet's *Déjeuner sur l'herbe,* and most interestingly perhaps, considering earlier discussions in this chapter, one of Blake's illustrations for Dante's *Divina commedia.* All of these pictures refer pointedly to the narcissistic qualities of art and its more than suspect power to capture truth. When Abel laments that he is an "homme du Moyen Age se survivant dans la Renaissance, incapable de l'appréhender" (3: 129), he also alludes to his painful awareness that pictures, like language, are no longer reliable. Thus, he confirms Ishmael's conclusion in *Moby Dick* that "there is no earthly way of finding out precisely what the whale looks like" and that "the only mode in which you can derive even a tolerable idea of his living contour, is by going a whaling yourself" (Melville 371).

In *Burning Water* and *Monsieur Melville,* postmodernist scepticism toward the mimetic ability of language has been placed at the service of defining the role of fiction in a post-colonial context. Thus, the dichotomy between the conqueror's code and that of the new territory is translated into the conflict of two different languages, with the narrator as the locus of assimilation in time and space. In a traditional definition of pictorial (simultaneous) as opposed to textual (sequential) encoding, Bowering and Beaulieu make use of the static qualities of pictures to help define that locus. In *Burning Water,* the critique of image-making serves to heighten Bowering's critique of the strategies of imperialism. In Beaulieu, pictures offer a temporary arrest of the writer's imagination, but, precisely because he places such faith in the power of pictures, Abel Beauchemin despairs doubly whenever he becomes aware of the cultural burden most images carry as well. Anxious to create the epic that will make Québec a visible nation at last, Beauchemin succeeds only in conjuring up Melville's mute and transparent ghost. A contemporary writer's imagination is always in danger of becoming a claustrophobic *musée imaginaire;* in Beaulieu's understanding, the imagination of the Québec writer operates in a museum of European and American artifact from which a Canadian aesthetic must be assembled. He exposes the dilemma further in the concluding volume of the *Voyageries, Una* (1980), where Beauchemin's fascination with Melville is critically reviewed through the eyes of a precocious child. Revealingly, the illustrations in *Una* are children's drawings, unrestrained by aesthetic rules, but also already components of a flawlessly printed book.

2. *Trieste and* Burning Water

Dear George,
… Smaro and I are proposing to go to Greece for a few weeks. We are not going to Trieste, even though Smaro would like to go to Trieste and look there for you writing another captain, a captain who might or might not be Captain Vancouver. We are going to Greece in July, but we are not going to Trieste.…
Bob

Dear Bob,
Well, I dont know why you coudna gone to Greece THRU Trieste, I mean go to Trieste, and then take the bus or train or boat or plane to greece. Or just stay in Trieste. I was in the U. of Wash bookstore the other day, and there was a remainder of somebody's book on Italo Svevo, and for some fool reason I didn't buy it, but I opened it to see two turn of the century pictures of Trieste, and as usual they lookt just like 1981 photos of Trieste.…
GB
(George Bowering papers, NLC)

In search of a place where he can write his book without distractions by telephone, mail, pub, and wife, the narrator of George Bowering's *Burning Water* escapes to Trieste where – like his West Coast Indians – he waits "for a shape to appear out of the fog" (Bowering 1980b: 17), that is to say for inspiration to materialize. Reviewers of Bowering's book have generally been irritated by the sections dealing with Trieste (and those referring to Florence, Venice, Guatemala, and Costa Rica), because they appear to be superfluous interpolations distracting the reader from the main narrative (see Giltrow; Scott). Yet Trieste and the territory surrounding it are so strongly associated with crucial developments in modern history and literature as to make its very name into a quotation. Bowering, as his correspondence makes amply clear (Bowering papers NLC), is aware of these associations and makes extensive but subtle use of them in his novel. In *Caprice*, he remains faithful to his obsession with the city: one of the main characters, the multi-lingual Luigi Martino alias Lause Martens, spent his childhood in Trieste.

There are few causal connections between Vancouver's Pacific North West and the narrator's Trieste. Instead, the novel further develops Bowering's exploration of the collage and uses "nets of images and analogies" (Marinetti: 86) in keeping with one of the book's main concerns, namely to challenge the conventions of realism and the omniscient narrator as the fossils of a self-confident era and to revive instead the medieval idea of the cosmos as a system of "correspondences and coincidences, ... analogies and allusions, strongly imply[ing] the existence of an ultimate reality that man cannot comprehend" (French 90), except that then, the Great Chain of Being was believed to be firmly held by the hands of a benevolent God, whereas now such correspondences – their traditional symbolism obsolete – may well be reminders of an existential void. As Olson suggested in *The Special View of History* (1970), "a teleology of form as progressive was the hidden assumption of the old cosmology, and Void is what's left when Kosmos breaks down as the interesting evidence of order, Man falls when that purpose falls, and so Void is the only assumption left" (Olson 47ff).

Una città morta?

Trieste is an Italian port located along a "spill of white mountains and foggy water" (Bowering 1980b: 8) across the Adriatic Sea from Venice. Its present political status is the result of embittered fighting among Germans, Yugoslavs, and Italians – involving the United Kingdom and the United States as intermediators – during and after the Second World War, and of riots, in 1953, against the allied military government.[3] When Italian troops entered the city in 1954, they put an end to political upheaval in a territory that "Romans and Venetians, Hapsburgs and Fascists had fought for and signed papers for" (8). During the Middle Ages, Trieste had been overshadowed – sometimes eclipsed – by the magnificence and mercantile success of its neighbour Venice which invaded its territory periodically, last as late as in 1570. In 1382, however, Trieste placed itself under the protection of Leopold III of Hapsburg, an action initiating almost uninterrupted Austrian rule until the end of World War I when Italy occupied the city following a secret agreement between France, Russia, and the United Kingdom. Under the Hapsburgs, Trieste became an important port and, following the loss (in 1859) of Austria's northern Italian provinces, the Empire's chief access to the Mediterranean. In rivalry with the northern port of Hamburg, large shipping companies like Lloyd Triestino settled in the city, banking and entrepreneurial dynasties flourished, the colourful ships of the Austrian fleet congregated in the bay, and tonnage increased steadily following the opening, in 1869, of the Suez Canal; the first ship to pass the as yet unfinished canal was a steamer from Trieste, the *Primo*. Trieste was given a railway in 1857; broad streets, large squares and handsome neoclassicist buildings in Vienna's *Ringstrasse* style were put up on land reclaimed from the sea, after Maria Theresia and Joseph II of Austria had already made efforts in the previous century to modernize the city by pulling down the old fortifications and encouraging the building of the Città Nuova. To this day, however, old buildings and streets remain in Trieste to remind the visitor of the city's age dating back to the time of the Roman Empire.

The population, grown from 5,700 in 1719 to 229,510 in 1910, included Italians, Slovenes, Croats, other Austrian subjects like Germans and Hungarians and a sizable group of foreigners from Greece, Turkey, and elsewhere. Particularly active in the professional life of the city were members of the Jewish community, numbering about 6,000 in 1910. Like the Riva degli Schiavoni in Venice, the streets of Trieste swarmed with men in Levantine and Slav costumes, illustrating the city's role as Austria's gate to the East and a kind of watershed between Western and Oriental civilization. "A Trieste on sent le voisinage de la Turquie," noted Stendhal, appointed French consul there in 1831 by Louis-Philippe, "des hommes arrivent avec des culottes larges, sans aucun lien aux genoux, des bas et le bas de la cuisse nu; un chapeau qui a deux pieds de diamètre et une calotte d'un pouce de profondeur. Ils sont beaux, lestes et légers. J'ai parlé à cinq ou six; je leur paie du punch, ce sont des demi-sauvages aimables; mais leur barque sent diablement l'huile pourrie, leur language est une poésie continuelle" (Dollot 34).

Despite its flourishing business, visitors to Trieste often found its cultural life dull and provincial. Chateaubriand, on his way to Jerusalem in 1806, considered its proximity to the East not half as inspiring as Stendhal was to concede it to be, "Cette ville, régulièrement bâtie, est située sous un assez beau ciel, au pied de montagnes stériles: elle ne possède aucun monument. Le dernier souffle de l'Italie vient expirer sur ce rivage, et la barbarie commence...." (Chateaubriand 771). Stendhal complained about its vulgar obsession with money, while the Irish novelist Charles Lever, British vice-consul in Trieste between 1867 and 1872, wailed that "of all the dreary places it has been my lot to sojourn this is the worst" and snobbishly deplored that the Austrian officials had failed to exert a refining influence on the city's Greek and Jewish *nouveaux-riches* (quoted in Stevenson 280). Trieste's climate seemed to both exacerbate its dullness and to set its inhabitants' nerves on edge; in summer, it suffered from occasional earthquakes and the hot *scirocco* which would push the drains back into the sewerage system. In winter it was beset by fogs, rains, and the dreaded black bora which had been known to blow horse-drawn carriages into the sea; even now, in the months of January and February, ropes are placed at the street-corners for pedestrians to hang on to. Not surprisingly, the city habitually recorded an unusually high death-rate and acquired a certain notoriety for suicides and murders: the most sensational among these was the German art critic Johann Winckelmann's murder in 1768 by his homosexual lover. In a travel sketch dated 1979, Jan Morris notes, "the Trieste street-crowds ... do not smile too easily. They never whistle. They seem almost to be waiting for something to happen – nothing specific perhaps, nothing actually foreseeable, *just something*" (Morris 207), and a colleague at the University of Bologna fuelled my fascination with Trieste by announcing gloomily, "E una città morta!"

During the nineteenth century, with nationalism and republicanism gaining momentum all over Europe, the respectable façade of Triestino wealth barely covered violent differences among the city's various factions. Trieste's growing prosperity coincided with the expansion of the Irredentist movement, especially following the 1848 unrests, and citizens and police first clashed in 1868; Irredentist Italians loathed the Austrians, the Slavs disliked the Italians, the conservatives came to blows with the leftists. Because the Austrian population was in the minority (12,635 as compared to 118,959 Italians and 59,319 Slovenes and Croats in 1910), the Empire had an interest in keeping strife alive; in other words, it wanted to "divide and rule" and supported its goal by never allowing Trieste to have its own university. Members of the Austrian royal family were perpetually threatened by assassination in Trieste; there were – as Isabel Burton, Sir Richard

Burton's wife, reported – "bombs on the railway, bombs in the gardens, bombs in the sausages" (Burton 18). The words "patria," "libertà" and "Italia" were forbidden at the theatre, and Irredentist newspapers such as *L'Independente* and *Il Piccolo della sera* were frequently raided by Austrian officials.

During the last few years of the Austrian Empire, Trieste seemed to be a mirror-image of the fatal contradictions afflicting the Hapsburg monarchy and, in a sense, much of Western Europe as a whole. Its explosive ambiance of imperialist wealth and cosmopolitanism, of geriatric bureaucracy, nervous *ennui*, and simmering anarchism made Trieste a kind of fulcrum between traditionalism in politics and art on the one hand and modernity on the other. The conflict expressed itself well in the lives of several members of the Austrian royal family. Stripped by constitutional monarchy of most of their presumably God-given superiority over their subjects, the Empress Elisabeth and her son Rudolph realized that their intelligence and talents would not suffice to guarantee them a place of excellence in a democracy, and attempted to cloak their growing awareness that they were parasitical anachronisms with eccentric or megalomaniac behaviour. Elisabeth's brother-in-law, the Archduke Maximilian, tried to escape the boredom of an aimless existence by accepting the crown of Mexico in 1864 where he was shot by firing squad in 1867. He embarked on his fatal journey in the small harbour of Miramar, a white neo-gothic castle near Trieste, a retreat he had built for himself and his bride Charlotte of Belgium. Miramar – its location and interiors – are a reflection of Maximilian's dreams and delusions. The "archdupe's" study is modelled on the Norvara, the ship that was to take him to Mexico; the library boasts 6,000 volumes and marble busts of Shakespeare, Homer, Dante, Goethe; the chapel mimics Jerusalem's Church of the Holy Sepulchre. Exotic trees, including firs from Spain and the Himalaya, palms from California and cypresses from (of all places) Mexico, surround the castle.

It seems appropriate that Maximilian's relative, the Archduke Ferdinand, was returned to Trieste as a flower-bedecked corpse following his assassination in Sarajevo; his death signalled, among other radical changes, the end of royal dilettantes in search of a people to rule and, considering that the daughters of Louis XV and members of the Bonaparte family had lived in exile in Trieste, made the city into a sort of cemetery for Europe's dying aristocracy.

A watershed of time and space, Trieste is appropriately associated with the literary equivalent of the historical developments outlined above. Thus, the city features in fictions ambiguously poised between realism and modernism: Trieste serves as a pivotal point in Daniel Deronda's gradual discovery of his Jewish roots, and Thomas Mann's Aschenbach briefly stops in Trieste before embarking, from Pola, for Venice in a sea voyage which is to initiate his increasing alienation from his former methodical self.

Even more crucially, Trieste is linked to key texts of modernism: Umberto Saba's *Il Canzoniere* (1921), Rilke's *Duino Elegies*, James Joyce's *Ulysses* (both published in 1922, the *annus mirabilis* of modern literature) and Italo Svevo's *La Coscienza di Zeno* (1923). The city has retained its fascination also for postmodernists such as John Berger (*G* [1972]) and Daniele del Giudice (*Lo Stadio di Wimbledon* [1984]). All of these texts express a distrust of teleological history, a Thucydidian "search for object facts and their causal connectedness" (Faas 43), and instead return to Herodotus' concept of history as "*parataxis* in which the words and actions reported are set down side by side in the order of their occurrence in nature, instead of by an order of discourse, or 'grammar'" (Olson 1964: 41). Poems or novels associated with Trieste are often written from a *flâneur* or transient visitor's perspective, with the city's neo-classicist façades forming a sharp contrast to "the sheer appreciation of the instant moment" (Lawrence 86). James Joyce, an accomplished *flâneur*, taught – with interruptions – English in Trieste between 1905-1915, and compared the city to his native Dublin, perceiving parallels in the contrast between their size and provincialism, in their distinctive dialects, and in the disproportion between the ruling and the ruled (Ellmann). Rilke composed the first two of his *Duino Elegies* during an extended stay at Duino Castle near Trieste in 1904-05 under the patronage of Marie, Princess of Thurn and Taxis, herself a living symbol of the cosmopolitan and elegant but irretrievably doomed European aristocracy. Italo Svevo and Umberto Saba, although both born in Trieste, were exiles in their own city because of their Jewish background and, despite their love for the places of their childhood, often wrote about their hometown with a mixture of detachment and affection. Svevo's *La Coscienza di Zeno*, later acclaimed by Alain Robbe-Grillet as a forerunner of the *nouveau roman*, adopts the bastardized Triestino dialect to describe the trivial problems of a mediocre man (notably his efforts to quit smoking) with the same care and detail granted to complex moral problems in the traditional realist novel. Saba roams about the old town finding "the infinite that is humility" in "a prostitute with her sailor, the old man / who stands there cursing, and a stammering crone, / a soldier seated at the fishfry stand, a jilted girl who cries out terribly / for love, for love" (Saba 23). Daniele del Giudice's *Lo Stadio di Wimbledon* pays postmodernist homage to the era of Saba and Svevo by piecing together, through the testimony of survivors, the story of Roberto 'Bobi' Bazlen, supporter of Svevo, Saba, and Montale and himself the most talented, erudite, and mysterious author of the Triestino *bohème*. Yet Bazlen never wrote a book of his own because life became his work of art, a conclusion the fastidious narrator of *Lo Stadio di Wimbledon* draws with some hesitation because it sounds like a cliché, before he experiences in his own work the difficulties of approximating the absolute. Obsessed with charting and measuring devices as the inadequate means of capturing an aleatory reality, del Giudice's narrator strongly resembles Bowering's Captain Vancouver, although Bowering would not have been familiar with *Lo Stadio di Wimbledon* when he wrote his book. But *Burning Water* does allude to Berger's *G.*, a book attempting to retrieve Trieste's "organic" and "sensual" history as well as analyzing its political situation. Bowering also refers to the eighth "Duino Elegy" ("Wer hat uns also umgedreht ..."), and *Burning Water*, which in the original manuscript featured extensive quotations in German from the *Elegies,* may be called an *étude* for the *Kerrisdale Elegies.* Rilke's poem speaks of man as someone who says forever farewell to the natural world surrounding him because he insists on subjugating it to his intellect, a flaw afflicting both Trieste's capitalists and officials and Bowering's own George Vancouver.

"Only the distractions were real ..."

The narrator of *Burning Water* flees from Vancouver to Trieste expecting it to be a vacuum, ideal for concentrated work: "the weather would be too poor to promote lying on the beach, the city so dull that one day's walk would take care of the sightseeing, and he didn't know a soul (or body) within a thousand miles and knew only a close relative of the language" (18). But instead of temporarily settling in a blank time and space, he has – as we have seen – chosen a spot teeming with literary and historical associations, its dullness the mask of exhaustion and disillusionment, not the symptom of an uneventful past. The city refuses to be a study-room only and demands its own attention: "He thought ... he would enter the job without any distraction. Instead, he found ... that only the distractions were real and seized upon" (26). As he also becomes a *flâneur*, observing Trieste's people ("For instance the guy with no legs in the rain on the Corso Italia, with his leather peaked hat" [23]) and responding to the abrupt juxtapositions of the ancient and modern ("A block from my hotel was a Roman theatre, across from the police station" [10]), he is no longer singlemindedly preoccupied with his book. His body, too, unsettled by travel, demands attention: he feels sick, is sleepless, thinks of nothing but food.

His own physical needs bring about a somewhat comical first encounter between George Vancouver and Trieste's Hapsburg past: the narrator devours meal after meal of *salsicce con krauti*, inspired – perhaps – by Vancouver's sauerkraut diet, and by Trieste's hybrid traditions. With physical discomfort and loneliness, the narrator's personal history and "home-territory" begin to emerge: "In Trieste there was no mail. Vancouver, B. C., was proceeding day by day independent of his help or even knowledge. Was his wife alive? Was his daughter? Did his house stand?" (62). Adriatic coast and Pacific North-West, past and present, George Vancouver and George Bowering, demand equal attention, and if the narrator had hoped to create a traditional historical novel – and "all the confusion" does make him long briefly for the "good old days, when the realist novelist just had to describe the setting and introduce into it the main characters" (23) – his hopes are shattered in Trieste. Realism, a literary convention suggesting that the *zeitgeist* of any one period can be resurrected in its speech patterns, costumes, and customs, becomes an unacceptable formula in a place where a multitude of histories (including the narrator's own), each one with its own code of truth, interpenetrate each other. As in *La Coscienza di Zeno*, the traditional hierarchy of the significant (that is, officially recorded) and the trivial (that is, private, unproclaimed) is abolished.

Looking out across the water to Trieste from Venice – "To where the grey sky joined with the grey Adriatic a few hundred yards away" (54), Bowering's narrator also contemplates the ever-widening fissures between reality and art. The edge between water and land, "that meeting / completely clear / completely free of death" (Bowering 1970b: 14), gives off the promise that such a linkage may be possible, that phenomena and language may indeed be matched. As Bowering's narrator walks away from the Lido, however, an Italian phrase crosses his mind: "Mi mostri la barca di salvataggio, per favore." Summoned to help him cross the gap between reality and art, this rescue-craft is the vessel of imagination, reminding us that boats and piers have been favourite metaphors for this process since Joyce referred to a pier as a "disappointed bridge" in *Ulysses*, since Robbe-Grillet, in *Le Voyeur*, described a landing ferry, inching toward the mole with infinitesimal precision, and since Fowles positioned his elusive heroine on the wind-swept tip of a pier in *The French Lieutenant's Woman*. The Karst surrounding Trieste, its steep slopes with their "chasms, gulleys and loose rock" (Berger 1972: 247) plunging toward the sea, is uninhabitable, not to be subdued by geometry; the city in front of it seems a small, precarious structure claimed from rock and sea, its geography confirming its role as historical and cultural borderland. Bowering's narrator builds his

The *Burning Water* Trilogy 101

fiction like a sea-side city, knowing full well that he is constructing it on shifting sands and that the underlying chaos can never be fully conquered. The narrator's efforts duplicate Captain George Vancouver's to chart the Pacific West Coast. Vancouver, a man used to "a civilized arrangement of chalk cliffs to mark an edge" (106), is confronted with "sharp straight lines, tree and cliff, mountain and sea" (20).

In constructing his fiction, Bowering's narrator relies on his reader's collaboration to "carry him, keep him afloat" (174), offering a number of clues to guide him. Among these are mythological allusions, particularly those pertaining to the myth of Daedalus and Icarus. One part of their story is concerned with the labyrinth that the artificer Daedalus built as a prison for the Minotaur. Like other cities in modern literature – Joyce's Dublin, Musil's Vienna, Döblin's Berlin, Dos Passos' New York – Trieste becomes Bowering's metaphor for a structure so ingeniously planned that it is a deadly trap even for the designer. Trieste's imperialist past, reflected in the neoclassicist façades of its banks and palazzi where "every window and doorway has its Corinthian pilasters, architrave and pediment" (Berger 1972: 255), pushed the city into anarchism. Trieste's fate – anarchism and violence – foreshadows Captain George Vancouver's. Instead of using neoclassicist architecture, he attempts to trap reality in the labyrinths of his maps and charts, and borrows Peter Paul Rubens' and Benjamin West's historical tableaux and the baroque music of Handel's Coronation Anthems for the same purpose. Official art assumes the pose of spontaneous expression, but – according to John Berger – it is an attempt to disguise and legitimize brutal materialism. Vancouver's efforts too breed violence. One of his officers condescendingly allows a "noble savage" to fire a pistol. The Indian shoots "the table that Puget's chart was on, and the chart along with most of the table was blown into shreds" (131). Vancouver himself is shot by his surgeon, Menzies, and drowns in the sea he tried to conquer as a captain.

Another part of the Daedalus/Icarus myth describes their flight from the realm of Minos, and Icarus' death by drowning after venturing too close to the sun with the wings his father had fashioned out of feathers, twine and wax. Like the myth of the labyrinth, this story archetypically captures both the exhilaration of creation and its preposterousness. Bowering's narrator repeatedly refers to the advantages of air travel enabling him to be in Vancouver and Trieste (a city associated with worldwide communication) within a relatively short period of time. The technology of modern-day travel permits Bowering's narrator to look at the ground with – as it were – a giant lens allowing him "to glimpse the space surrounding [his own life]" (Berger 1975: 202). He sees the sun above "the fog of Milan and the fog of Trieste ... because the Italian pilot of the DC-9 took us all up into the bright shine for a moment's steep bank" (10), and thus realizes one of George Vancouver's dreams who, at one stage in his exploration of the West Coast, takes off on a visionary flight across the Canadian continent, cruising aboard the *Chatham* through "miles and miles of cumulus" (134). In attributing exceptional importance to air-travel, Bowering furthermore confirms Filippo Marinetti, Gabriele d'Annunzio, Gertrude Stein, and John Berger's conviction that the elimination of viewer-oriented depth (and the resulting simplification and flattening of shapes) contributed to shattering the Renaissance perspective and to ushering in Cubism. "As I looked at objects from a new point of view," writes Marinetti, "I was able to break apart the old shackles of logic and plumb lines of the ancient way of thinking" (Marinetti 88), that is, revive the medieval preference for analogy in which connections are created through semblance rather than cause and effect.

Yet, the flight is dangerous. Bowering's narrator feels close to death while on a plane, and the sun above the clouds over Trieste could always be the sun that melted Icarus's wings. From the beginning of *Burning Water*, when the *Chatham* and the *Discovery* appear out of the fog like "two immense and frighteningly beautiful birds upon the water ... their huge shining wings ... folded and at rest" (14), flying and sailing are closely associated with the albatross and with Daedalus's guilt: one of the ships cruising with Vancouver on the North West Coast in 1792 was named the *Daedalus*. Although the surgeon Menzies shoots an albatross, cutting it "into several new shapes, examining it for everything from diet to diseases of the talons" (87), the bird remains a symbol of Vancouver's ambition and downfall: "Will you want me round your neck till I fall?" (258) he shouts as Menzies prepares to kill him.

Trieste, as we have seen, is a city in which multiple linguistic traditions have struggled for power, and a great part of its oppressors' guilt consists in enforcing the "language of the overseer." (Berger 1972: 346) Even before 1918, street-names were in Italian in apparent deference to the linguistic majority, but the language of the law remained German. After 1918, Slovenes were expected to bow to Italian as "the language of law, insult and demand;" the defiant use of Triestino in Svevo's *La Coscienza di Zeno* was a first step toward rejecting any one language as prescriptive and therefore oppressive. Bowering's novel too is a collage of different languages, different literary styles and quotations. None of these, however, is permitted to dominate the others. The Indians, for instance, refuse to engage in "dumb-talk" or the diction of noble savages unless they find it strategic to do so. One of them replies in the metaphors expected of him to Vancouver's question about the location of the North-West Passage, "It is as many suns as we all have fingers on our hands.... Many portage. Many days eating chickens on the flat land past the highest mountains" (143-144). The narrator adds, "this last was an inspired guess" and thus anticipates the Indian's final, almost compassionate – and completely unmetaphorical – comment, once Vancouver has left for his fanciful quest, "I saw that he had come to buy something" (144).

Trieste in *Burning Water* functions as an especially complex quotation among numerous others from literary sources (Shakespeare, Coleridge, Melville, Thackeray, Rilke, Berger) and documentary ones (Vancouver's and Menzies' log-books). None of these quotations totally encapsulates Bowering's novel, nor do his allusions to myth. "Il faut savoir que tout rime,"[4] muses the narrator at one point, but also admits "To tell the truth, it *was* different [in Trieste]. It was lonelier alone in the damp" (44). Similarly, the allusions to Trieste in *Burning Water* may open a number of avenues into this book, but, as no coast-line repeats exactly another, they can do no more than contribute to a multiplicity of possible readings.

3. Caprice

... while pre-realist fable, fantasy, myth, and the unnatural narrator have re-emerged in the literatures of the older world, Canadians intent on discovering themselves and exploring their time have been slow to welcome the unreliable and the capricious in their writing, to respect the author who invents rather than obeying.

("A Great Northward Darkness: The Attack on History in Recent Canadian Fiction," *Imaginary Hand*)

Toward the end of her quest for her brother's murderer, Caprice asks herself: "So why was she following their trail with no known destination? She was writing because she was looking forward to the last stanza" (Bowering 1987: 49). Following after the first sentence, "She was writing" comes as a surprise, and the reader wonders if "writing" is perhaps a slip of the pen for "riding," much as Caprice originally misreads a verse in Goethe's *Faust* as "build words" instead of "build worlds" (21). There are many misunderstandings and puns in *Caprice*. All of them are highly significant, and the exchange of "writing" for "riding" may be one of the most illuminating for the book as a whole. The dustjacket advertises the novel as "an action-packed novel about a woman," "a clever takeoff of the standard Western," and "a great old-fashioned yarn." All of this is true, and *Caprice* has become Bowering's only "popular" book to date. At the same time, however, it is also an allegory of writing and reading, and Caprice's restless pursuit of Frank Spencer and Louis Groulx through the B. C. Interior is one of the most successful and complex translations of his "poetics of unrest" which Bowering has achieved to date. The middle portion of the as yet uncompleted *Burning Water* trilogy, *Caprice* is a suitable last text to consider in a study which has been concerned with the encyclopedic openness of Bowering's *oeuvre*. Moreover, this is a book which extensively explores the politics of vision, and it confirms and expands many of the observations that have already been made on that subject.

Caprice is a poet who, with the exception of occasional work on a poem with the opening lines "Toujours le bon Dieu reste muet," has largely deferred her writing until her mission has been completed because "here I am not a poet. I am a sister" (31). She does, however, write her verse on the land, an activity not altogether unusual in a country where poems come rolling by tied to tumbleweeds (21). Throughout, her solitary ride on a black horse through the sun-bleached land is likened to the tracing of black marks on a white surface. The marks are light, in keeping with Caprice and Cabayo's respect for, and harmonious integration into, their natural environment: there are "purple lakes" (6) on the horse's hide, and Caprice, whose "long smooth back [has] a valley down the middle" (75), moves "like a cougar" (59). The allegorical fusion of "writing" and "riding" becomes especially apparent as Caprice approaches Deadman Falls for her final meeting with Spencer and Groulx, but here, with Cabayo replaced by an ordinary mare and Caprice's extraordinary height stunted because she has lost her heels, the meandering lines of her long ride are suddenly channeled into a narrow road, "as if she were being conducted through an enormous natural loading pen toward her last journey" (252). The ambiguity of "loading pen" is surely intended, as it not only refers to the loading pens which channel cattle into boxcars for processing (just as the conclusion of a quest formally channels all the disparate elements into "resolution"), but also alludes to the potential destructiveness of both guns and pens. Logically, an Indian child complains to his teacher that his pen "does not understand [his] words" (175), and one particularly manipulative writer, the Austro-Hungarian journalist Arpad Kesselring, has his gold-nibbed pen crushed by one of his more reluctant subjects, an incident comparable to the destruction of George Vancouver's maps in

Burning Water. The text of Caprice's encounter with Spencer and Goulx is seemingly inexorable, written "black on white" by the conventions of the Western, but the rushing waters of Deadman Falls speak a language of their own. Groulx and the horses, "black against the white" (255), drop in the ravine when a ledge (a line?) gives way "without disturbing the speech of the water."

Numerous reminders of the oceanic past of the land anticipate this undoing of a human plot by a dynamic natural environment, and acknowledge that the land has a script of its own:

> ... along with the thin lichen you will likely spot the signature of a small shelled creature from under the sea.... You will read the first writing of the Thompson Valley, a story left by a departing sea that never saw a sailor. (34)

Even relatively clichéd expressions such as "you would have seen late-morning sunlight *flooding* ... the wide grassy valley" (1) and "the evening sun still *bathed* the range land above it" (32, emphasis mine) help to constitute the "fluid" story of the land, a story encapsulated in a variation of William Carlos Williams/Phyllis Webb's "The sea is also a garden," namely "the dry land is also a garden" (166). Williams' and Webb's verse provides yet another link to *Burning Water*, where it is also quoted and where Vancouver's attempt to impose the narrative of his own psyche and of his imperialist mission on the west coast ends with his death by drowning.

If Caprice is a writer and reader, she is also a poem herself. As a text, she is almost as magic as the land upon which she inscribes her story; in the scene at Deadman Falls, the "braided descent" (257) of the water evokes her braided hair, and "the precipice edge ... was the same shape as the scar on her cheekbone" (255). The many eyes that follow hers try to read her "surfaces," and there are almost as many details about her freckles, her blushing, the light down of hair on her skin, and the changing highlights on her hair as there are descriptions of the brushland. Not even her lover "reads" her, however, and he points out to her that she is "living in a different alphabet" (76). Her attacker attempts to break her enigmatic code and impose his by ripping off her shirt and baring her skin, a scene whose violence matches the sailors' sexual attacks on the Indians in *Burning Water*. It is also significant that in both cases the attack comes from behind, avoiding the gaze of the victim, and Caprice's violation is mirrored in her "eyes [which] were not in control of the seeing" (185). Caprice's champion, Everyday Luigi, pays for his "cavalleria" by suffering painful bruises to his skin and even losing half of his face. He only survives as well as he does because of Doc Trump's care, who reads bodies as patiently as Caprice reads the land, "a kind of writing perpetrated by parts of the body most people never see or even think of" (167).

Resembling the magic words and drawings in the Indians' stories, Caprice is a poem in which there is almost no gap between *signifiant* and *signifié*. The young boy in spectacles, Bowering's *alter ego*, does catch her once treating him "disingenuously" (196), and she speaks "in a language she was borrowing" (214) to a sod-buster's wife, but these are incidents which make her less of a sign and more of an unpredictable human. For most of the time she is what she seems, and while her unconventionality may be considered capricious, there is also a remarkable, almost mythical, stasis about her, captured in the formulaic incantations of her physical beauty that accompany virtually all of her appearances in the novel. Caprice's name is part of that incantation, and it radiates beyond her into a text practically teeming with words starting with her trademark C.

By contrast, the names of the other characters are ostentatiously marked as arbitrary, ranging from Luigi Martino who is forced by political circumstances to change his name from Lause Martens, or Frank Spencer whose viciousness is not revealed by a "dangerous-sounding nickname" (13), to the naming of Indian children after an elk because their "fathers have pretended to see an elk at the birth of their children" (56). There is occasional "name-calling" to adjust the *signifiant* to the *signifié*, as in Caprice's exchange with Arpad Kesselring whom she contemptuously calls both "Mr. Kiss" and "Mr. Kesselringworm," or in Mr. Soo's hilarious conversation with the hospital receptionist to whom "Woo" is clearly a generic name for all Orientals:

"Yes Mr. Woo."
"Mistah Soo."
"Thank you, Mr. Woo. You are very kind." (138)

The arbitrariness of names is particularly foregrounded in the anonymity of the first and second Indian, the first and second constable, the first and second boy, the first first baseman and the second first baseman, "names" which do not prevent any of these – particularly not the first and second Indian – from having a recognizable presence of their own. Words are explored within the historical field which has shaped their meaning, and their claim to absolute truth is further relativized in dialogue with members of another culture. Thus, Luigi unsuccessfully attempts to explain the concept of "cavalleria" to the Indians, and the narrator's etymological treatise on the feudal origins of the word "game" is complemented not only by descriptions of baseball games, but also by the Indians' comparison of their own traditional sports with baseball, and by Roy Smith and Caprice's playful exchange over his pedantry:

"Are you supposed to do this before a match?"
"Game. A game."
"*Ah oui, un game.*" (49)

The narrator is particularly on the lookout for words which, like "game," are freighted with imperialist and prejudicial overtones; "tribe" is such a word, as are "anthropology" and "Chinese community." The wittier characters in *Caprice* dismantle such words by punning, while the dimmer or more recalcitrant ones freely misunderstand them, confusing "a patchy [country]" with "Apache," or "motivation" with "motive nation." As in *Kerrisdale Elegies,* Bowering frequently marks such slippages by introducing another language or accent, as in "Sam Ann Hell" from "San Angel" (89), or "Missed [y]a so" from "Mistah Soo" (138).

In a book where spoken and written language comes under close scrutiny, "silent" languages like gestures, facial expressions and sign language logically play a special role. Metapoetic adaptation of the taciturn Western hero, Caprice mystifies her surroundings with her wordless and unreadable smiles, and her opponent wants to break her not only by raping her, but also by "mak[ing] her beg for it" (29). But like her name and her beauty, Caprice's body language is an original text and differs sharply from the intertextualities that shape the gestures of others in the book. Like spoken language, gestures are subject to conflicting codes, therefore prey to misunderstanding, and there are almost as many physical puns in the book as there are verbal ones. The lower half of his face shot away and his head "full of pain and language" (165), Luigi communicates by sign language, learning a particularly complex version from the Indians and promptly "mispronouncing" a crucial phrase. And in a country where a cowboy's hat and the way in which that hat is raised tell a story of their own, such gestures can also lead to inadequate readings. Thus, Charlie Westoby, the stagecoach driver, mistakes a hold-up for a friendly greeting and blithely thunders on past "four eyes staring with disbelief" (94).

Sign language requires close visual observation. The main focus of the book is an exploration of that process, and all other concerns are subsumed by it: in the first scene of the book, the Indians spy Caprice for the first time, and by comparison and contrast with available vocabulary attempt to find a term to describe the apparition, but they are "not sure [they] can find the words" (2). Simultaneously, the Indians try to catch slippery fish from the creek, an activity paralleling their linguistic experiment, linking the book to the previous volume, and introducing the water motif mentioned earlier: it is probably no coincidence that Caprice, the subject of the Indians' search for words, later enjoys trout at Mr. Kearns' "Fish House."

There are eyes looking, staring, darting, roving, gawking, spying, and scanning in *Caprice,* and there are spectacles, field glasses and cameras to help them. Occasionally, the looking becomes so intense that it resembles physical contact, and clichéd expressions such as "sore eyes" or "within eye-shot" (freely adapted from "ear-shot") repossess the aggressive meaning that is their due. Luigi, the "Eye-talian," even seems like a walking eye, the more so since, after the shooting, his "big gooey eyes" have to approximate the many languages he knows. Far from establishing the "truth" about a knowable universe as empiricism would have it, vision is shaped by influences of which physiology is only one, and the intertextual complexities of gestural language are further compounded by the limitations of the eyes which attempt to decipher them.

The opening chapter and several others throughout the book view a specific scene through different sets of eyes whose vision has been affected by their owner's age, his ethnic and occupational background: there are "ordinary English eyes," "ordinary Yankee eyes," "ordinary Scottish eyes," "ordinary eastern eyes," the eyes of "an extraordinary journalist," "famous Indian eyes," and the eyes of "an infirm old uncle." All of these sets of eyes, penetrating as they may be, are limited by the specific properties of human vision and inferior to the extraordinary eyes of an eagle or hawk. Space, in *Caprice,* is constructed in discontinuous layers of vision, which cannot possibly emanate from one single person (or animal), and the reader must assume that the narrator, like Coyote, is given to metamorphosis. Moreover, as the narrative persistently uses the second person singular, the reader is urged to participate in the various transformations. In so doing, the narrative breaks up the complicity that informs realist fiction where the reader agrees to see things the narrator's way. This complicity postures as an esthetic convention but is grounded in oppressive political strategy. Their amiability notwithstanding, the Indians' close visual scrutiny of the whites is, above all, an act of self-protection conducted in the partisan spirit of "Do not assume all the invader's ways, but make use of the particulars that will bring strength to the people" (128).

The *Burning Water* Trilogy 109

Such watchfulness must be exercised with all of the white man's artifacts, and as in *Burning Water*, Bowering attacks the imperialist propaganda informing oil paintings of natural or historical grandeur, particularly their popular, hence widely disseminated, versions, the "sentimental painting[s] such as one was likely to find in an Alberta hotel lobby" (243). In *Caprice*, Bowering is, however, especially concerned with photography and, in Archie Minjus, creates his own addition to the ever-growing army of photographers in Canadian literature. As Bowering reminds us, photography was a particularly effective and ambivalent tool in creating a national self-image for Canada, for it provided an encyclopedic record of the new nation's varied populace and achievements (Kröller 1985). As a scientific invention, it carried the cachet of unassailable truth, and poses and perspectives already entrenched in oil painting were newly legitimized. Thus Indians were photographed projecting "the kind of dignity one was expected to show in the ceremonial meetings and the photographs" (56), not taking into account that pose and costume might in fact violate the Indians' codes of self-representation (Thomas). Such pretense is brutally stripped away in photographs recording the reading of the land for its service to the Empire, but even here, the conventions of oil-painting remain in effect: "A typical photograph would depict several men in rude clothes standing beside a sluice in front of a hill that had been stripped of trees and bushes and anything a poet might claim to be impressed by" (99). In this photograph, man poses as the "winner," a cruder version of the foreground figures surveying a groomed parkland in Claude Lorrain's landscape tableaux or the token tree stumps inserted in many landscape paintings commissioned by the Canadian Pacific Railway.

Archie Minjus, a late nineteenth-century reincarnation of ship surgeon Menzies, knows that he plies a potentially destructive trade:

... he had killed over five hundred Shushwap Indians. He had killed the McLean boys. He had taken the cover off his lens and sent the surviving Overlanders to their grave. Each was a shadow that spoke from dying lips. (147)

But Minjus is also an extraordinary photographer. He not only creates a portrait of Caprice that pleases her, but he is also a patient reader of surfaces, an ability which in one scene links him to Doc Trump, reader of bodies: "The photograph-maker had his own bedside manner. Doc would grump and mutter, but he would agree to have the emanation of light off his body make its mark on the immortalizer's emulsion" (166). His work has taught Minjus to perceive the world as a series of discrete images, each of which maintains its independence and integrity in relation to those surrounding it. His esthetic is, in fact, in advance of the technology available to him, for his work anticipates the snapshot photography of Cartier-Bresson:

> When Cartier-Bresson pickt up a small, fast camera for the purpose of snapping art, he changed the course & meaning of photography throughout the world, the picture frame gone, & the 'decisive moment' here when we can enter it, the art said good bye to the parent, came out & changed the way we look at the world, & the way we think about it. (Bowering 1980e: 7-8)

It is significant that Minjus's momentous portrait of Caprice is not described in any great detail, because this would fix the "invention" (149) in the black-and-white of print, dragging it from "the shadow ... where breathing things lie at midday" (147).

The anachronism embodied in Minjus's snapshot work implicitly comments on, and subverts, the time-space construct perpetuated by the *camera obscura* and its successor, the photographic camera. John Berger points out that "spatial perspective is closely connected with the question of time," that the "fully articulated system of European landscape perspective ... only preceded by a decade or two Vico's invention of modern history," and that the idea of the vanishing point also implied "that of unilinear time." (Berger 1980: 83). As if to illustrate Berger's point, time and space are inseparably linked in *Caprice*. Characters see time as they "look at the end of spring and the beginning of summer" (15), and they pay "attention to shadows, to know what time it was" (1). But as the "point-of-view" of the book is composed of various visions, so too time is layered into natural and chronological time, codes often in conflict with each other: "old folks around here always got into disputations about when things happened.... That was because ... time had just turned into a sluice of seasons" (9). The book as a whole, although riddled with ostentatious historical markers, frequently violates chronology, and Stan Dragland has pointed out some of the book's historical and idiomatic inconsistencies (Dragland 1988). Anachronistic of course is also the presence of the two Indians who presided over *Burning Water* as well, of Bowering's *alter egos*, George Delsing and the young boy in spectacles, and of the literary intertextualities, two of which – *The Double Hook* and *Tay John* – tie the book closely into the "Sheila Watson canon," Bowering's counter-proposal to the official canon. Like the polysemic spaces in the book, these violations of unilinear time are an esthetic as well as a political commentary. In its sharp division into past, present, and future, time is turned into a

The *Burning Water* Trilogy

commodity to be spent at the discretion of the ruler. The past is consigned to nostalgia, and the old Indian points out to his disciple that "[the white man] is going to make us live in the past, and his notion is that we do not need much room to live in the past. In fact his notion is that we are the past" (113). Similarly predetermined is the future as travelling photographers entrap images of the economic "future" of the land. The present seems only significant as a link between these two. The book sets about restoring the present, more specifically the present continuous, in Minjus' snapshot photographs and in the texture of its language: the old Indian's speech about the past contains the Steinian repetitions with which Bowering characteristically undermines the humanist/realist time-space construct.

Bowering's abhorrence for "popular" books notwithstanding, *Caprice* is a remarkable achievement, and if this book cannot persuade some of his more reluctant readers that the self-reflexivity of his writing is grounded in responsibility and humaneness, nothing can.

CHAPTER SEVEN

The Making of a Literary Reputation

I like photographs rather than paintings or drawings, rather than art, to decorate my books. On the cover or inside, I prefer photographs. Photographs happen now, and then, now and then. But art always happens when. No matter how active, art comes from somewhere like eternity and is pointing its nose, and ours, toward eternity. The photograph is "taken" or made in perhaps one five-hundredth of a second. Think what a second is to eternity, and then think of five hundred possible photographs in that time. My books are that far away from the perfect. But look how much light there was available in one five-hundredth of a second! It is not that a photograph is more real than a drawing – it is only that you know it was made more by light than by you. I keep hoping that that is true about my books – or something that feels like that. Writing can be so nice when it is a snap. (*Errata*)

No approach to Bowering's work would be valid without taking into account the controversy surrounding his work and person from the start. Bowering has persistently subjected his literary and personal reputation to the same deconstruction as his work. As a result, reviewers have sometimes paid closer attention to his personal eccentricities than to his writing; thus, a 1987 profile in *Books in Canada* spends an inordinate amount of space on these, and even Sheila Watson, who has been a very attentive reader and collector of his books, remembers being first impressed by his appearance: "he was dressed completely in black leather – an enigma like the enigma which his subsequent activities as a writer were to reveal him to be" (Watson 9). His biography, one may argue, is *one* element in the collage of literary genres with which he has experimented over the years, among them the *Künstlerroman* in the abortive Delsing novels, the *nouveau roman* in *Mirror on the Floor*, the historical novel in *Burning Water*, the Western in *Caprice*, and the thriller in his most recent novel, *Harry's Fragments* (1990). To Bowering, his life too has embodied "the impossible ideal [of the collage]: the loss of both subjectivity and objectivity in the ceaseless flow of entities" (Kuspit 47). A good illustration of Bowering's concept of self are the photographs on some of his books, especially *Mirror on the Floor* and *Kerrisdale Elegies*, which continue and parody a tradition of self-dramatization developed by his mentors Walt Whitman, William Carlos Williams and Jack Kerouac. In the first edition of *Leaves of Grass*, Whitman's portrait casts him in the role he celebrated in "Song of Myself," as "Walt Whitman, an American, one of the roughs, a Kosmos ...," although he later became strongly identified with another photograph showing him as an ancient bearded prophet (a portrait Cesare Pavese held responsible for the misinterpretation Whitman suffered at the hands of his European reviewers). W.C. Williams intended to run no such risk when he rejected his photograph by Man Ray as too decadent and "un-American" in pose and style, but he did approve of Charles Sheeler's detached portraiture. Jack Kerouac continued the tradition with the picture on the dust jacket of *On the Road* which showed him "tough-looking, brooding, unshorn, and unshaven with a silver crucifix around his neck" (Cook 72). Bowering's photographs go a step further than his predecessors': here, the authorial mystique is often ironized, even self-destructive. On the back of *Mirror on the Floor*, the young author is shown soberly attired in suit and tie, gazing pensively into the distance. But one side of the photograph is torn along the edge, and it may well be this ragged edge that the author is staring at. He appears less as a detached creator of his work than as a fragment contained in it, a strategy repeated twenty years later on the cover of *Kerrisdale Elegies*, where a torn and blurred portrait of the poet tensely looking across his shoulder "exceeds its margin threatening to erase Bowering's name." Smaro Kamboureli argues that "the author's visage is foregrounded; his name is held in disbelief" (Kamboureli 1987: 10), but everything about the image suggests that it too "is held in disbelief." One is reminded of Oskar Mazerath's experiments with his passport photographs in *The Tin Drum* when, grown intensely wary of the legitimacy of humanism after the events of the Holocaust, he cuts the images up and rearranges his features to convey a sense of fragmentation and insignificance.

As anthologizers in search of reliable biographical data have had ample occasion to find out, Bowering has subjected his life and work to similar rearrangements. There is considerable uncertainty surrounding the place and date of his birth, which have been variously given as 1935, 1936, 1937, 1939 and Penticton, Kelowna, Keremeos, Princeton, even "Alberta.": "I was born many times in different places" (37) he suggests in *Autobiology*. He has variously adopted the pseudonyms of "Helmut Franz," "E.E. Greengrass," "Erich Blackhead," and "Edward Pratoverde," later shortened to "*Ed Prato* so he would be more contemporary and more

Canadian" (Miki ix), all of which have allowed him to lead a multiple existence as lyric poet, alleged redneck conservative, and immigrant author. As the latter, he successfully submitted poems to Pier Giorgio Di Cicco's collection *Roman Candles: An Anthology of Poems by Seventeen-Italo Canadian Poets* (1978) and provided the editor with a fictive biography, which contains one of the first incidents of Bowering's obsession with the city of Trieste: "My parents came here from Trieste in 1951, and I was born a year later, in Trail, B.C." (Miki 134). Grown wary, I even suspected him for some time of having invented his friend Bob Hogg so as to have an equivalent to Shelley's indispensable Thomas Hogg.

It would be easy to dismiss Bowering's role-playing as a harmless joke, or else as evidence of the narcissism with which he and TISH have been frequently charged. The archivist of his papers at the National Library seems to have come to just that conclusion when she labelled a folder documenting some of Bowering's more spectacular pranks "Silly Pseudonyms." However, the root of Bowering's role-playing is serious: from the beginning of his career, he has sought to escape the single-person perspective, and posited his self as an object as much in need of exploration as its environment. "My name is not Bower or Bowered," he writes in *Errata* (1988) – and surely *that* title is significant too – "It is Bowering, so I suppose that the second word I ever learned to read looked like a present participle. Maybe I learned from the start of the written language to think of myself as an ongoing verb." (7).

Bowering has been careful to maintain a fluidity in the overall "chronology" of his opus. Librarians have found it difficult to verify the existence of some of the books he claims to have published, although he obtained ISBN numbers for them, and one exasperated victim responded in kind when he reviewed one of Bowering's non-existent books. Complex incongruities, however, also affect his extant work. On various occasions, he has outlined distinct critical phases which are to serve the reader as guidelines through his books:

1 A lyric phase, represented by such early volumes as *Sticks and Stones* (1963), *Points on the Grid* (1964), *The Man in Yellow Boots* (1965) and *The Silver Wire* (1966). Bowering posits the end of this "apprenticeship" phase during his years in Montreal (1967-71) which "took me out of my poetry." His "last lyrics" appeared in *Another Mouth* (1979) and in *The Concrete Island: Montreal Poems 1967-71* (1977), a smallish volume which seemed to reflect in its very appearance the atrophy of "these desperate poems, seeking the lost assurances of a young poet's method."

2 A "symphonic phase" with an emphasis on the long poem, a form he

promoted as editor of *Imago* (1964-74). Early suites of poems were *Baseball, a Poem in the Magic Number 9* (1965), *Rocky Mountain Foot* (1968), and *George, Vancouver, a Discovery Poem* (written 1967, published 1970), *Genève* (1971), *Autobiology* (1972), *Curious* (1973), *Desert Elm* (1976) and *Allophanes* (1976). In many of these, his focus shifts from a concern with place to an exploration of time, both personal and ancestral.

3 A phase – initiated by *A Short Sad Book* (1977) – concentrating on fiction and critical prose, although his arguably most important suite of poems, *Kerrisdale Elegies*, also appeared during this period. Short story collections, *Protective Footwear* and *A Place to Die*, were published in 1978 and 1983 respectively; the first two volumes of the *Burning Water* trilogy, *Burning Water* and *Caprice*, followed in 1979 and 1987; and books of criticism, *The Mask in Place, A Way With Words, Craft Slices, Errata* and *Imaginary Hands* in 1982, 1985, and 1988 respectively.

To each one of these phases, Bowering assigns roughly a decade of his life, and he seems to consider it indecorous when preoccupations of an earlier phase filter into a later one. "[E]specially for somebody who had been deracinated, it makes sense, *in your twenties*, to write lyric poems in which the configuration of the place is so important to your finding out who you are *in the twenties*. I think *in the thirties* you tend to get out of place and more into time" (88), he said to Caroline Bayard and Jack David in 1978, later adding: "*Genève* was another way of getting to that [= the concept of collaboration], it seems to me a more sensible way *for my age at the time* (emphasis mine)" (89). On occasion, he responds with irritation to questions about interests he considers *passé*. Interviewed about *Burning Water*, he said: "The historical novel was a problem that needed solving given the context of things that I'd been writing so I'll never write another historical novel" (Leitch 1980).

Bowering's outline for a "history" of his work, first published as a preface to *In the Flesh* (1974), is quoted in full in Robin Blaser's introduction to *Particular Accidents: Selected Poems* (1980), and it serves as a guideline to Peter and Meredith Quartermain's entry in *The Dictionary of Literary Biography* (1986) as well. Still, there is evidence that Bowering's scheme has to be considered with caution, and that Bowering the poet has found ways to outwit Bowering the critic. Reg Berry formulates the problem well: "Bowering's writing career divides into three fairly distinct periods, depending on which creative drive is turned on. In each period, there are also important bursts from the other side, to use a metaphor from his favourite game, baseball" (Berry 1984: 3). Bowering's papers indicate that fiction was his first obsession, and that the *Burning Water* trilogy, especially *Caprice*, provides a link to an older, monumental project temporarily abandoned when its first volume, "Delsing," was not accepted for publication, although fragments found their way into *Mirror on the Floor* (1967) and several short stories. The envisaged scope of this *roman-fleuve* may be gathered from a "Note to the Publisher's Reader" appended to "Delsing," which is well worth quoting in full, because it throws light on the encyclopedic ambition of Bowering's *oeuvre*:

> The present is ... projected as a seminal portion of a much larger work contemplated for the future, a work that has been in process for a number of years. Parts not appearing here are already written ..., further parts are in the process of being written, either in notes, whole first-drafted segments, or as included in the novel ... on which I am now working. I have about 2000 pages worth of fiction planned for continuation of the large work, several novels already promised to my next few years' work (Bowering papers NLC).

Instead of confirming a sequential development neatly divided into temporal and spatial stages, Bowering's many publications often seem splinters of a multi-layered *Gesamtkunstwerk*, the "scatter[ed] fragments of the exploded gods," as he writes in *Allophanes* (1976).

Vitriolic comments about the institution of history indicate that Bowering suspects it to be a way of "ascertain[ing] facts and ... arrang[ing] them into an incontrovertible theory, to change story into system" (Bowering 1988b: 5), and he has variously undermined attempts, including his own, to turn his work into a completed system. He has, for instance, created alternative "histories." In one of these he methodically lists his works by title and date of composition, combining them in groups of 100 (Bowering papers NLC). Each group is named: poems from 1955-58 bear the title "The Immaterialist," followed by "The Adventurist, 1958-60," "The Psalmodist, 1960-61," "The Projectionist, 1961-62," "The Subsensualist, 1962-63," "Misbehaviourist, 1963-64" and so forth. Despite its methodical appearance, this list by numbers is as aleatory as the alphabetical order Bowering uses in *Craft Slices,* in imitation of Roland Barthes's procedure in his autobiography *Barthes par lui-même* (1975). The titles suggest a series of self-ironical masks, as "The Gin & [Chthonic], 1976-78" or "The Haruspex, 1981-82" make particularly clear. Masks provide Bowering, who entitled a collection of essays *The Mask in Place* (1982), with alternative "histories." Thus, after having assured Bayard/David that he considers lyric poems inappropriate for his age, he announced, "I still publish lyric poems under a pseudonym because I'm not a lyric poet any more" (84).

Bowering's playfulness has been intriguing to critics interested in his

The Making of a Literary Reputation

contribution to Canadian postmodernism (see, for example, Hutcheon 1988), but it has been odious to nationalist critics who consider it anarchist, narcissistic, in short "American," a reputation exacerbated by Bowering's association with TISH, whose penchant for American poets such as Robert Duncan, Robert Creeley and Charles Olson is well-documented. Until the warm reviews which greeted *Kerrisdale Elegies* (1984) and *Caprice* (1987), Bowering's literary reputation was largely one of "an internationalist viper in our midst" (Bowering 1974d: 12). When he received his first Governor General's Award in 1970, he invited his teacher Warren Tallman to attend the ceremony; security was especially tight because "officials expected nationalist students to protest the presence of an American on the Canada Council jury, namely Warren Tallman" (Miki 291).

A tone of moral outrage pervades criticism of his most controversial books. *Burning Water* (1980), which won Bowering his second Governor General's Award, was even granted a *succès-de-scandale*, but the latter only confirms the controversy stirred up by much of Bowering's work and personality throughout his career. The strongest indictment of *Burning Water* came from librarian and historian W. Kaye Lamb, who – as a former Dominion archivist – found Bowering's manipulation of history morally objectionable: "Bowering has not only violated the basic facts of Vancouver's career, he has bespattered his pages with numerous errors of fact that are both pointless and needless" (Lamb A5). Equally severe was an editorial in *Canadian Literature:* "[the book] constitutes a clever idea in technique, all of which ends in a historical violence, all of which is marred by crude anachronisms and deliberate contrivance, and none of which is therefore transformed beyond cleverness into literature" (New 1981: 20). And finally, *Books in Canada* published a review so extravagantly negative that another critic screening the responses to *Burning Water* (Pache) was led to believe that the reviewer had deliberately and self-ironically donned the guise of an arch-conservative *literatus:* "This is a truly ugly book, ugly in spirit as in appearance (computypeset, in a golden and brown wrapper like a chocolate bar, a blotchy imprint giving off a foul chemical odour), a book possessing no authentic voice, no authentic sense of time or place, a book adrift in the author's fancy...." (Scott 9).

Although perhaps not ostensibly so, such criticism reads Bowering's deconstructionist version of Vancouver's travels as an act of treason against an episode in Canadian history which, together with other voyages and explorers' tales, doubles as a founding myth. Roy Daniells for one compared Alexander Mackenzie's voyages with the Argonauts' search for the Golden Fleece,[1] and similar analogies have been suggested over the years by Thomas Guthrie Marquis (1911), A. J.M. Smith (1965), and T.D. MacLulich (1979) (Gross 11). A text such as *Burning Water* is suspected, and rightly so, of sabotaging the enterprise of a cohesive Canadian mythology, hence a cohesive national identity, a concern much fueled by the activities of the Centennial decade. The construction, and re-confirmation, of a Canadian mythology in the encyclopedias, anthologies and literary histories of the sixties was bolstered by an emphatic re-assertion of Arnoldian cultural values. These were formulated in such diverse statements as the Massey Report (1951) which expressed a marked preference for high culture over popular culture, suggesting that the former would prove a bulwark against American predominance (Litt), and in Dennis Lee's moving manifesto "Cadence, Country, Silence: Writing in Colonial Space" (1972). Lee describes how the burden of a double heritage, British and American, temporarily yet severely paralyzed his creativity, but driven to ally himself with one of them, he and other nationalists ranked "European" values above "American" ones. Partly out of revulsion with the United States' involvement in Vietnam, Lee turned toward his loyalist forebears whose beliefs taught "that reverence for what is is more deeply human than conquest of what is" (76). The importance of historical tradition was re-affirmed, and with it the "Tory mode" (MacLulich), elements of which persist in the writing of nationalist authors even as experimental in other ways as Lee himself and Margaret Atwood. In assuming the role of "custodians of a higher standard of political morality and cultural purity than that prevalent in the United States" (MacLulich 10), these writers opt for language as "a vehicle for considered reflections." According to MacLulich, the tone of the "Tory mode" at its most extreme is "formal, educated, and precise [and] presents carefully arranged results of prolonged cogitations" (17). Peter Quartermain, in a superb retrospective analysis of the controversy surrounding TISH, correctly suspected that the collective "offend[ed] a sense of order and propriety deep-rooted in genteel Canadian letters" (78), but it is worth pointing out that this "sense of order and propriety" also prevails in writing which was considerably more than "genteel."

It is illuminating to apply a comparative perspective to this compulsion to assign specific moral values to different forms of discourse, because both sides often claim virtues so similar that their conflict makes sense as a problem of cultural semiotics rather than as an expression of axiomatic truths. A particularly complex and appropriate example is Black Mountain College, an experimental institution in South Carolina (1933-1956).

The Making of a Literary Reputation 119

Duncan, Creeley, and Olson were all associated with the College at one time or another, and the TISH collective became so strongly identified with it that visitors to Vancouver are reputed to have come looking for it there. Black Mountain evolved from early affiliation with Bauhaus ideology under Josef Albers's leadership to an emphatic assertion of American aesthetics under Charles Olson; the names of its most distinguished students and teachers read like a roll-call of the American *avant-garde:* John Cage, Merce Cunningham, Buckminster Fuller, Willem de Kooning, Franz Kline, Robert Rauschenberg. In attempting to delineate American values as distinct from European ones, Black Mountain College rehearsed the dichotomies ironically later also used by Canadian nationalists and, in a complete reversal, by Europeans. Thus, the American faction at Black Mountain – later consistently blamed for imparting a belief in individualism and anarchy to the members of the TISH group – posited as a counter ideal to European elitism, snobbery, and self-absorption "a cooperative democracy in which the discovery of meaningful aspects of the self could take place through activities designated as socially useful." They "viewed that orientation, with its emphasis on 'doing good,' as particularly American" (Duberman 25f.). Conversely, prominent German intellectuals greeted Leslie Fiedler's late 1960s lecture "Cross the Border – Close the Gap" with open animosity: now that American pop-culture was widely perceived as overwhelming European tradition, authors such as Martin Walser fought to uphold the "European" ideal of social and political commitment which they felt was being lost to the "American" narcissism infecting their post-modern colleagues Peter Handke and Rolf Dieter Brinkman (Walser). Yet another reversal occurs within the context of some post-colonial criticism; here "readerly" discourse equals legibility by, hence subservience to, the dominator, while "writerly" discourse affirms his rejection (see Ashcroft, Griffiths, Tiffin).[2] Against this background, the open animosity expressed by militant nationalists toward TISH's phenomenological approach, preference for open forms, and self-reflexive poetics reveals itself to be a part of the general post-war struggle for cultural supremacy. Only Sheila Watson, in her Preface to *West Window: The Selected Poetry of George Bowering* (1982), has so far attempted a brief, but impressive, synthesis of Bowering's place in that process.

To militant nationalists, TISH's "American" poetics discredited members of the collective well beyond their student years, and it may be argued that the furor created by *Burning Water* was only a late fallout. The conflict is, moreover, exacerbated by an East-West tension, in which representatives of the East have assumed the role of mentors for an unruly brood of western poets. Keith Richardson's polemic *Poetry and the Colonized Mind: TISH* (1976) defined the "Canadian tradition" as "formally conservative, intellectually rather than experimentally founded, and concentrated somewhere in Eastern Canada" (Cooley 100). Even an avant-gardist such as Louis Dudek who, together with Raymond Souster, is often cited as one of TISH's sources of inspiration, adopted a paternalist pose when he wrote an invective against Bowering's *The Silver Wire* (1966), which may well be a classic in Canadian review literature. Dudek condemned Bowering for using "tasteless orthographics" and took him to task for "revel[ing] in intimacies of sex": "Physical demonstrations belong in the lunatic asylum, not in imaginative literature" (Dudek 81). Most significantly, he objected to Bowering's use of the enjambment and even re-wrote a poem to correct it; his emphasis on "nuances of meaning" rather than "the obvious" suggests that Dudek here too values argumentative sophistication over the colloquial:

Bowering actually says that 'what is written down is a score.' He may have discovered this on his own; or he may have picked it up in Vancouver in the summer of 1962 from one of Dudek's lectures (it's a long-standing principle with me). What does it mean? That the arrangement of a poem is a guide for the real or imagined voice, also (as I must have said in Vancouver) that it does not emphasize the obvious, but brings out nuances of meaning. In Bowering's poetry I find the enjambment merely disturbing, erratic and eccentric (Dudek 82).

Partly in response to such patronizing posturing, Bowering and other former members of TISH have persistently *equated* modernism with patriarchy, described it as "an elitist, formalistic, anti-democratic and anti-terrestrial movement" (Davey 19), and failed to acknowledge its full experimental and ethical range. Much of Bowering's writing has even been formally adapted to the anticipated critical onslaught from modernists and nationalists. The metafictional interpolations in early stories such as "ReUnion" ("Oh What a boring story, nothing happens" [*Protective Footwear* 16]) have blossomed into "long collage poems... stuffed with nugatory asides" (Whalen 34) which are in sharp contrast to his self-contained early imagist lyrics. *Uncle Louis* incorporates the voice of a "snotty Toronto reviewer" (Miki 59); "A Preface" (*Another Mouth*) presents a dialogue between "Canadian Tradition" and George Bowering, which is modelled on a similar exchange, in *Paterson*, between William Carlos Williams and an interviewer; and the original manuscript of *Burning Water* features an opinionated reader by the name of Mr. Jones who can be trusted to slam the book down frequently, exclaiming "All right! I will not read another word!" (Bowering papers NLC).

The Making of a Literary Reputation 121

These caricatures have led critics to the conclusion that Bowering's desire to establish "an intimate, teacherly relationship" with his reader are often "vitiated ... by a[n] impatience with [his] (assumed) stupidity" (Whalen 33). Jeanette Lynes categorizes the readers who are Bowering's favourite targets as "plot mongers," "censors," and "critics." She also identifies his fear of "the institution or academy" as the place where most readers are trained to perform "reader vandalism" (Lynes 68). Yet Bowering has taken measures to protect the text or to resuscitate it when it has been violated. Thus, in *Craft Slices*, he "de-institutionalizes" his frequently anthologized poems by telling their mundane stories of origin ("Anthology Poems") and salvaging them from the nationalist interpretation to which, despite his wicked reputation, they have been subjected. In "A Transcanada Poetry Quiz With no Questions about Snow" (*Another Mouth*), he further quite logically elevates a multiple choice quiz about Canadian poetry to the status of a poem because the poem itself has been submerged in extraneous concerns, and he has exploited his famed enjambments to create the caricature of a positively diabolic high school teacher in "A Poem for High School Anthologies":

This will be serious, literature,
& Canadian, you'll have to look out for
the author's intentions, & also
his tricks, his puns, his jokes, the things
he is doing to make it
difficult
& hence worthwhile. Right?
(*Another Mouth*)

Nor has Bowering protected only his own works from violation. He has consistently championed authors ignored by the nationalist canon, and he has established an alternative "Sheila Watson canon," so named after its most prominent member (*Craft Slices* 55). His best critical essays, such as his reading of Robert Kroetsch's *Stone Hammer Poem* ("Stone Hammer Narrative"), Margaret Avison's poetry (*A Way with Words*), bp Nichol's *Journeying & the returns* (*Imaginary Hand*) are closer to religious exegesis than to scholarly analysis, as they combine an attentive explication of the properties of the text with a fraternal respect for its identity: even in TISH, Bowering compared the writing of "a paper / on the Brontë genius" with the dissection of animals, "the signs of severed brains / along the sinkboard" (Davey 1975: 3).

It cannot be ignored, however, that Bowering is fully immersed in the very academic institution that he often professes to despise. His role as teacher, administrator, and frequent delegate to Canada Council committees, has provided him with considerable power, and he wields it with a self-assurance which can be troubling at times. He was probably only half joking when he wrote in a burlesque sketch about the former TISH poets:

> The original Brown Mountain Poets (or at least the Vancouver ones) are now in positions of power at many Canadian universities, and some of us serve on Canada Council committees. In every way we can even try to mould the poetic minds of young writers, including those brought up in the snow belt. (*Craft Slices* 15)

Amusing as such a parody of existing power structures may be, it appears that here Bowering's dialogism is a disguised monologism (Whalen 37),[3] for his insistence that open discourse be privileged to the exclusion of others ultimately leads to the same institutionalization he so castigates elsewhere. If Bowering, then, has taken pains to practise, in his life and work, the "indeterminate yet insistent flow" of the collage (Kuspit 47), he also falls prey to its inherent paradox: it is made up of disparate fragments which together form a new and unexpected configuration, but each of which also contains powerful elements of its traditional origins:

> The implication of the collage, which appears arbitrary and so disturbing, is that it is extraordinarily difficult to suspend the given meanings, the expected forms, the obligatory order, the traditions (whether personal or social) by which we live, and to establish a creatively open horizon. (Kuspit 53)

Notes

Introduction
1. Also see Red Lane (1975).
2. Also see Kamboureli (1985).
3. I disagree with Spanos's view of the detective story as grounded "in the comforting certainty that an acute 'eye' ... can solve the crime with resounding finality by inferring causal relationships between clues which point to it" (Spanos 151). It could be argued that, on the contrary, the detective story, E.A. Poe's in particular, conveys the resistance of things to being rationally analyzed.

Chapter One
1. I have borrowed this chapter heading from Harris 196.
2. On the Vancouver Poetry Festival, see Bergé and Franklyn.
3. On *Swift Current*, also see Nischik.
4. See Mathews 1982 / 83; also Jackel.
5. For a detailed reading of this poem, see Peter and Meredith Quartermain.
6. For a detailed analysis, see Smith.

Chapter Two
1. See Ricou (1987) for a detailed reading of this poem.
2. See Cavell (1988) and Kröller (1987).

Chapter Three
1. Also see Perloff (1987): 172-200.

Chapter Five
1. See Fülleborn, Engel.
2. For a particularly sensitive response to this aspect of the poem, see Dragland (1986).

Chapter Six

1. See for example, Sarduy (1973) and (1974). A similar connection between postmodernism and the baroque is discernible in Québec literature; see Kröller (1985a).
2. Hastings questions Bowering's metaphorical uses of homosexuality as a form of "reverse repression," which entrenches homophobic prejudices while seeking to indict racial bigotry.
3. Information on Trieste has been compiled from: Powell (1977); Morris (1970); Robida (1974); Cox (1977); Furbank (1966); Ara, Magris (1982); *Encyclopedia Britannica*.
4. According to Bowering, the quotation is from Wols (pseudonym for Otto Alfred Schutz-Battmann, a *tachiste* painter).

Chapter Seven

1. Roy Daniells, "A Position Paper apropos of the Proposed Cultural History of Canada," unpubl. ms. (1972?), quoted in Gross (1982).
2. The list could be continued. Loriggio, for instance, speaks of the "nihilistic jocundity of deconstruction" and argues that it "will not serve [ethnicity] better than the strict, stoic vision of the structuralist for whom man and meaning are all rule governed" (Loriggio 60).
3. It should be pointed out, however, that Whalen's criteria for successful poetry preclude appreciation of much of Bowering's writing. Writing about *At War with the U.S.*, Whalen uses a phrase which is anathema to Bowering's poetics: "*The poet's sufficient control over his highly charged subject* matter saves him ... from self-conscious asides to the reader (emphasis mine)" (34).

Works by George Bowering

For a detailed bibliography of works by and about George Bowering, see Miki.

1. Manuscripts

Bowering papers, National Library of Canada

2. Published Works

1963 *Sticks & Stones.* Vancouver: Tishbooks.
1964a *Points on the Grid.* Toronto: Contact.
1964b "Dance to a Measure" in Bowering (1988c): 137-148.
1965a *The Man in Yellow Boots/El hombre de las botas amarillas,* with translations to Spanish by Sergio Mondragon, Mexico City: Ediciones El Corno Emplumado.
1965b "Universal and Particular: An Enquiry into a Personal Esthetic," *Aylesford Review* 7.1: 219-236.
1966 *The Silver Wire.* Kingston, Ont.: Quarry.
1967a *Baseball: A Poem in the Magic Number 9.* Toronto: Coach House.
1967b *Mirror on the Floor.* Toronto: McClelland.
1967c "Letter to the Editor." El Corno Emplumado 22: 141.
1968a *Rocky Mountain Foot: A Lyric, A Memoir.* Toronto: McClelland.
1968b "Why Reaney is a Better Poet" in Bowering (1982f): 24-36.
1969a *How I hear "Howl"* in Gervais 216-229.
1969b *The Gangs of Kosmos.* Toronto: Anansi.
1969c "Sitting in Mexico." *Imago* 12.
1969d *Two Police Poems.* Vancouver: Talonbooks.
1970a *Al Purdy.* Toronto: Copp.
1970b "George, Vancouver: A Discovery Poem" in Bowering (1976b): 11-42.
1971a *Robert Duncan: An Interview* by Bowering and Robert Hogg, Toronto: Coach House.
1971b *Touch: Selected Poems 1960-1970.* Toronto: McClelland.
1972a *Autobiology.* Vancouver: Georgia Straight Writing Supplement.
1972b *The Sensible.* Toronto: Massassauga.

1972c "Avison's Imitation of Christ" in Bowering (1982f): 5-23.
1971/72 "Delsing and Me," *Open Letter* 2.1: 157.
1973a *Genève*. Toronto: Coach House.
1973b *Curious*. Toronto: Coach House.
1973c *Layers 1-13*. Toronto: Weed/Flower.
1974a *At War with the U.S*. Vancouver: Talonbooks.
1974b *Flycatcher & Other Stories*. Ottawa: Oberon.
1974c *In the Flesh*. Toronto: McClelland.
1976a *Allophanes*. Toronto: Coach House.
1976b *The Catch*. Toronto: McClelland.
1976c *Poem and Other Baseballs*. Coatsworth, Ont.: Black Moss.
1977a *Concentric Circles*. Coatsworth, Ont.: Black Moss.
1977b *The Concrete Island: Montreal Poems 1967-1971*. Montreal: Véhicule.
1977c *A Short Sad Book: A Novel*. Vancouver: Talonbooks.
1978 *Protective Footwear: Stories and Fables*. Toronto: McClelland.
1979a *Another Mouth*. Toronto: McClelland.
1979b "14 Plums: An Interview," with Bill Schermbrucker, Sharon Thesen, David McFadden, Paul de Barros. *Capilano Review* 1.15: 86-107.
1980a *Uncle Louis*. Toronto: Coach House.
1980b *Burning Water*. Don Mills, Ont.: General.
1980c *Particular Accidents: Selected Poems*. Ed. Robin Blaser. Vancouver: Talonbooks.
1980d *Fiction of Contemporary Canada*. Ed. George Bowering. Toronto: Coach House.
1980e "Introductory Notes" in Bowering 1980d: 7-21.
1982a *Ear Reach: Poems*. Vancouver: Alcuin Society.
1982b *The Mask in Place: Essays on Fiction in North America*. Winnipeg: Turnstone.
1982c "The Painted Window: Notes on Post-Realist Fiction" in Bowering (1982b): 113-127.
1982d "The Poems of David McFadden" in Bowering (1982f): 1984-199.
1982e *Smoking Mirror*. Edmonton: Longspoon.
1982f *A Way with Words*. Ottawa: Oberon.
1982g *West Window: The Selected Poetry of George Bowering*. Toronto: General.
1983 *A Place to Die*. Ottawa: Oberon.
1984a *Kerrisdale Elegies*. Toronto: Coach House.
1984b "Stone Hammer Narrative" in Bowering (1988c): 171-183.

1985 *Craft Slices.* Ottawa: Oberon.
1985a *Seventy-One Poems for People.* Red Deer: Red Deer College Press.
1986a "bp nichol on the train." *Open Letter* 6.5-6: 7-20.
1986b *Delayed Mercy and Other Poems.* Toronto: Coach House.
1987 *Caprice.* Markham: Penguin.
1988a *Errata.* Red Deer: Red Deer College Press.
1988b "A Great Northward Darkness: The Attack on History in Recent Canadian Fiction" in Bowering (1988c): 1-21.
1988c *Imaginary Hand: Essays.* Edmonton: NeWest.
1988d "Extra Basis: An Interview with George Bowering" with Peter Quartermain and Laurie Ricou. *West Coast Review* 23.1: 52-73.
1990 *Harry's Fragments.* Toronto: Coach House.

Works Cited

Amaya, Mario (1970). "Canada: Jack Chambers." *Art in America* 58: 118-21.
Anon., (1987). "Simply Red." *Canadian Art* 4.3: 15.
Ara, Angelo and Claudio Magris (1982). *Trieste: Un' identità di frontiera.* Torino: Einaudi.
Art and Correspondence from the Western Front (1979). Vancouver: Western Front Publ.
Ashcroft, Bill, Gareth Griffiths, and Helen Tiffin (1989). *The Empire Writes Back: Theory and Practice in Post-Colonial Literatures.* London: Routledge.
Atwood, Margaret (1989). "Bowering Pie ... Some Recollections." *Essays on Canadian Writing* 38: 3-6.
Balkind, Alvin (1979). "Body Snatching: Performance Art in Vancouver – A View of its History" in *Living Art Vancouver*: 72-77.
Bayard, Caroline and Jack David (1978). *Out-Posts.* Erin: Porcépic.
Beaulieu, Michel (1983/84). "Le Canada existe-t-il?" *Nuit blanche* 11: 40-50.
Beaulieu, Victor-Lévy (1978). *Monsieur Melville*, 3 vols., Montreal: Vlb éditeur.
Beaulieu, Victor-Lévy (1976). *N'évoque plus que le désenchantement de ta ténèbre, mon si pauvre Abel.* Montreal: Vlb éditeur.
Bergé, Carol (1964). *The Vancouver Report.* New York: Fuckpress.
Berger, John (1972). *Ways of Seeing.* London: Pelican.
Berger, John (1975). *G.* London: Penguin.
Berger, John (1980). *About Looking.* New York, Pantheon.
Berger, John (1980). "Seker Ahmet and the Forest" in Berger (1980): 79-86.

Berry, Reginald (1984). "George Bowering: Line Drives from Both Sides." *Span* 19: 2-7.
Blaser, Robin (1980). "Introduction" in *Particular Accidents* (1980): 9-28.
Bollard, Margaret Lloyd (1975). "The 'Newspaper Landscape' of Williams' *Paterson*." *Contemporary Literature* 16: 317-27.
Bringhurst, Robert; Geoffrey James, Russell Keziere, and Doris Shadbolt, eds. (1983). *Visions: Contemporary Art in Canada*. Toronto: Douglas.
Buckle, Richard (1964). "Invitation to the Chance." *Sunday Times* 2 Aug.: n.p.
Burnet, David (1981). *Guido Molinari: Works on Paper*. Kingston: Agnes Etherington Art Centre.
Burton, Isabel (1893). *The Life of Captain Sir Richard F. Burton*. Vol. 2. London: Chapman.
Campbell, James (1989). "A Radical Agenda for Painting: A Genetic Chronology of Molinari's Early Years 1950-1961" in *Guido Molinari 1951-1961:* 19-39.
Castro, Nils (1972). "The Stormy History of *El Corno Emplumado:* An Interview with Margaret Randall and Robert Cohen." *Open Letter* 2, 3: 5-21.
Cavell, Richard (1988). "Horizontal Allegories: Text and Image in Atwood and Kiyooka." Unpubl. ms.
Chambers, John (1969). "Perceptual Realism." *ARTSCANADA:* 7-13.
Chambers, Jack (1972). "Painting, Perceptualism and Cinema." *Art and Artists* 7: 29-33.
Chateaubriand (1969). *Oeuvres romanesques et voyages*. Vol. 2. Paris: Gallimard.
Chateaubriand (1811). "Itinéraire de Paris à Jérusalem et de Jérusalem à Paris" in Chateaubriand (1969): 769-1343.
"Concrete Poetry" (1969) catalogue-folder, Fine Arts Gallery, University of British Columbia.
Conférences J.-A. de Sève 11-12 (1971). Montréal: PUM.
Cook, Bruce (1971). *The Beat Generation*. New York: Scribner.
Cooley, Dennis (1979). "Three Recent TISH Items." *Canadian Poetry* 3: 98-102.
Cox, Geoffrey (1977). *The Race for Trieste*. London: Kimber.
Curnoe, Greg (1967). "Statement" in *Statements:* 38-42.
Davey, *Frank (1972). From There to Here*. Erin: Porcépic.
Davey, Frank, ed. (1975). *TISH 1-19*. Vancouver: Talonbooks.
Davey, Frank (1976). "Introduction" in Gervais: 15-24.
Davey, Frank (1983a). "Surviving the Paraphrase" in Davey (1983b): 1-12.

Davey, Frank (1983b). *Surviving the Paraphrase*. Winnipeg: Turnstone.
Davey, Frank (n.d.). "The Fragmentation of Literature and its Audience in Contemporary Canada." Unpubl. ms.
Davidson, Michael (1981). "'To Eliminate the Draw': A Reading of *Slinger* by Edward Dorn." *American Literature* 53: 443-464.
Dollot, René (1948). *Autour de Stendhal*. Milano: Istituto Editoriale Italiano.
Dragland, Stan (1986). "The Bees of the Invisible." *Brick* 28: 14-25.
Dragland, Stan (1988). "Wise and Musical Instruction: George Bowering's *Caprice*." *West Coast Review* 23. 1: 74-87.
Duberman, Martin (1972). *Black Mountain: An Exploration in Community*. New York: Dutton.
Dudek, Louis (1967). Rev. of *The Silver Wire*. *Canadian Literature* 34: 80-84.
Duncan, Robert (1962). "For the Novices of Vancouver: August 25-28, 1962" in Davey (1975): 253-257.
Elder, Bruce (1981a). "Jack Chambers: Before Towards London and After." *Canadian Forum* 61.712: 16-17.
Elder, Bruce (1981b). "From Painting into Cinema: A Study of Jack Chambers' *Circle*." *Journal of Canadian Studies* 16.1: 60-81.
Faas, Ekbert, ed. (1978). *Towards a New American Poetics: Essays and Interviews*. Santa Barbara: Black Sparrow.
Farrell-Ward, Lorna (1983). "The Sixties: Alternating Currents" in *Vancouver: Art and Artists:* 132-141.
Feldman, Seth (1976). "The Hart of London." *Film Quarterly* 29.4: 54-57.
Fetherling, Doug (1987). *Documents in Canadian Art*. Peterborough: Broadview.
Fisher, Brian (1967). "Statement" in *Statements:* 44-51.
Fitzgerald, Judith (1983). "Curnoe Memory Paintings: Hospitals, Bicycles, Politics." *Globe and Mail* 20 Jan.: n.p.
Flint, R.W., ed. (1971). *Marinetti: Selected Writings*. New York: Farrar, Straus and Giroux.
Franklyn, A. Fredric (1963). "Towards Print: Excerpts from a Journal of the U of British Columbia Seminar." *Trace* 48-51: 277-284.
French, Marilyn (1976). *The Book as World: James Joyce's 'Ulysses'*. Cambridge, MA: Harvard UP.
Fülleborn, Ulrich, and Manfred Engels, eds. (1982). *Rilkes Duineser Elegien 3*. Frankfurt: Suhrkamp.
Furbank, P.N. (1966). *Italo Svevo: The Man and the Writer*. Berkeley and Los Angeles: U of California P.

Gagnon, François (1971). "Mimétisme en peinture contemporaine au Québec" in *Conférences J.-A. de Séve 11-12*: 39-60.
Gagnon, François (1976). "The 'Precociousness' of Guido Molinari." *ARTSCANADA* 33.210/211: 55-58.
Gervais, C.H., ed. (1976). *The Writing Life: Historical and Critical Views of the TISH Movement*. Coatsworth: Black Moss.
Giltrow, Janet (1981). Rev. of *Burning Water*. *Canadian Literature* 89: 118-120.
Ginsberg, Allen (1961). "Cézanne's Ports" in Ginsberg (1970): 12.
Ginsberg, Allen (1970). *Empty Mirror: Early Poems*. New York: Totem/Corinth.
Gross, Konrad (1982). "Kanada entdeckt seine Entdecker: Die Reiseberichte von 'fur traders' und 'explorers' und die Problematik der anglo-Kanadischen Gründungsliteratur." *Zeitschrift der Gesellschaft für Kanada-Studien* 2.2: 5-17.
Guido Molinari 1951-1961: The Black and White Paintings (1989) exh. cat. Vancouver: VAG.
Gunn, Thom (1988). Rev. of Robert Duncan, *Groundwork II*. *TLS*, Nov. 25-Dec. 1, 1988: 1299.
Gwyn, Sandra (1962). "Why Ottawa is Afraid of Art" in Fetherling (1987): 206-216.
Hale, Barrie (1976). "Talking Pictures." *The Canadian* 17 July: 12
Harris, Mary Emma (1987). *The Arts at Black Mountain College*. Cambridge, MA: MIT.
Harrison, Dick, ed. (1979). *Crossing Frontiers: Papers in American and Canadian Western Literature*. Edmonton: U of Alberta P.
Harrison, Keith (1967). Rev. of *The Silver Wire*. *Tamarack Review* 75.
Hastings, Thomas (1990). "The Sodomite's Body: Representations of Race and (Homo)sexuality in George Bowering's *Burning Water* and Thomas Keneally's *The Chant of Jimmy Blacksmith*." Unpubl. ms.
Heath Terrence (1983). "A Sense of Place" in Bringhurst et al. (1983): 44-77.
Hoffman, Katherine, ed. (1989). *Collage: Critical Views*. Ann Arbor: UMI.
Jackel, David (1983). Rev. of *Fiction of Contemporary Canada*. Ed. George Bowering. *Canadian Literature* 96: 151-2.
Kamboureli, Smaro (1985). "A Window Onto George Bowering's Fiction of Unrest" in Moss (1985): 206-231.
Kamboureli, Smaro (1987). "Stealing the Text: George Bowering's *Kerrisdale Elegies* and Dennis Cooley's *Bloody Jack*." *Canadian Literature* 115: 9-23.

Kisselgoff, Anna (1977). "A Dance Revolutionary on Broadway." *New York Times* January 16: 1.
Kiyooka – 25 Years (1975). Vancouver: VAG.
Knutson, Susan (1989). "Bowering and Melville on Benjamin's Wharf: A Look at Indigenous-English Communication Strategies." *Essays on Canadian Writing* 38: 67-80.
Kroetsch, Robert and Reingard Nischik, eds. (1985). *Gaining Ground: European Critics on Canadian Literature*. Edmonton: NeWest.
Kritzman, Lawrence D. (1981). *Fragments: Incompletion & Discontinuity*. New York: New York Literary Forum.
Kröller, Eva-Marie (1985a). "The Politics of Influence: Canadian Postmodernism in an American Perspective" in Valdès: 118-123.
Kröller, Eva-Marie (1985b). "Nineteenth-Century Photography and the Canadian National Image." *Zeitschrift der Gesellschaft für Kanada-Studien* 5.2: 83-92.
Kröller, Eva-Marie (1987). "Roy Kiyooka's *The Fontainebleau Dream Machine*: A Reading." *Canadian Literature* 113-114: 47-58.
Kuspit, Donald B. (1983). "Collage: The Organizing Principle of Art in the Age of the Relativity of Art" in Hoffman (1989): 39-57.
Lamb, Kaye (1981). "History As She Wasn't." *Vancouver Sun*. 29 May: A5.
Lane, Red (1975). "Big Benzedrine (an open letter to George Bowering)" in Davey (1975): 238-39.
Lauder, Scott (1982). "There's Also One About a Naked Ballerina." *Canadian Forum* 61.715: 6-9.
Lawrence, D.H. (1956). *Selected Literary Criticism*. Ed. A. Beal. New York: Viking.
Lee, Dennis (1972). "Cadence, Country, Silence: Writing in Colonial Space." *Liberté* 14.6: 65-88.
Lippard, Lucy (1987). "Watershed, Contradiction, Communication and Canada in Joyce Wieland's World." *Joyce Wieland (1987)*: 1-16.
Lista, Giovanni (1979). *L'Art postal futuriste*. Paris: Jean-Michel Place.
Litt, Paul (1989). "The Massey Commission as Intellectual History: Matthew Arnold Meets Jack Kent Cooke." *Canadian Issues* 12: 23-34.
Living Art Vancouver (1979) exh. catalogue. Vancouver: Western Front.
Lord, Barry (1981). "Let there be Darkness." *ARTSCANADA* 21: 21-27.
Lord, Barry (1968). "Swinging London." *Star Weekly Magazine* 13 Jan.: 19-20.
Lord, Barry (1974). *The History of Painting in Canada: Toward a People's Art*. Toronto: NC Press.
Lorrigio, Francesco (1987). "The Question of the Corpus: Ethnicity and Canadian Literature" in Moss (1987): 53-70.

Works Cited

Lowndes, Joan (1968). "Multi-happening of Michael Morris." *Vancouver Province* 27 Sept.: 10.

Lowndes, Joan (1983). "The Spirit of the Sixties: By a Witness" in *Vancouver: Art and Artists:* 142-151.

Lynes, Jeanette (1989). "Keeping the Vandals at Bay: George Bowering and Reader-Response Criticism." *Open Letter* 7.5: 67-79.

McLuhan, Marshall (1964). *Understanding Media: The Extensions of Man.* New York: McGraw.

Macdonald, Colin S., ed. (1967). *A Dictionary of Canadian Artists.* Vol. 3. Ottawa: Ontario.

MacLulich, T.D. (1981). "Colloquial Style and the Tory Mode." *Canadian Literature* 89: 7-21.

Magidson, Debby (1974). "The Art of Jack Chambers: Photography as Visual Reference." *Art Magazine* 6.19: 19-21.

Mandel, Eli (1979). "The Border League: American 'West' and Canadian 'Region'" in Harrison (1979): 105-21.

Marchand, Philip (1989). *Marshall McLuhan: The Medium and the Messenger.* Toronto: Random.

Marinetti, Filippo (1909). "Technical Manifesto of Futuristic Literature" in Flint (1971): 84-89.

Mathews, Robin (1982/83). "In Search of a Canadian Poetic: George Bowering *A Way with Words.*" *Canadian Forum* 62.723: 31-32.

Mayne, Seymour (1961). "Letter to the Editor" in Davey (1975): 53.

Melville, Herman (1851). *Moby Dick.* London: Penguin, 1980.

Miki, Roy (1989). *A Record of Writing: An Annotated and Illustrated Bibliography of George Bowering.* Vancouver: Talonbooks.

Miller, James E. (1979). *The American Quest for a Supreme Fiction: Whitman's Legacy in the Personal Epic.* Chicago: U of Chicago P.

Molinari. Guido (1976). *Écrits sur l'art.* Ed. Paul Théberge. Ottawa: National Gallery of Canada.

Molinari, Guido (1971). "Reflexions sur la notion d'objet et de série" in *Conférences J.-A. de Séve* 11-12: 61-80.

Moreno, César Fernández (1972). *America Latina en su Literatura.* 2nd ed. (1980). Buenos Aires: Siglo XXI.

Morris, Jan (1980). *Destinations.* New York: Oxford UP.

Morris, Jan (1980). "Trieste" in Morris (1970): 203-216.

Moss, John G. (1985). *The Canadian Novel: Present Tense.* Toronto: NC Press.

Moss, John G., ed. (1987). *Future Indicative: Literary Theory and Canadian Literature.* Ottawa: U of Ottawa P.

Nelson, Cary (1970-71). "Suffused-Encircling Shapes of Mind: Inhabited

Space in Williams." *Journal of Modern Literature* 1.4: 549-564.
Nemiroff, Diana (1981). "This is Great Art Because it is not Made by an American." *Vanguard* 10.8: 24-31.
New, William H. (1981). "Take Your Order...." *Canadian Literature* 89: 2-6.
New, William H., ed. (1986). *Dictionary of Literary Biography, Vol. 53: Canadian Writers since 1960.* Detroit: Bruccoli Clark, 1986.
Nill, Annegreth (1981). "Rethinking Kurt Schwitters: An Interpretation of *Grünfleck*" in Hoffman (1989): 225-251.
Nischik, Reingard (1984). "Literatur und Computer: Swift Current, die erste literarische Datenbank." *Zeitschrift der Gesellschaft für Kanada-Studien* 4.2: 136-140.
Olson, Charles (1964). Review of E.A. Havelock's *Preface to Plato*. *Niagara Frontier Review* (Summer 1964): 40-44.
Pache, Walter (1985). "'The Fiction Makes Us Real': Aspects of Postmodernism in Canada" in Kroetsch and Nischik: 64-78.
Perloff, Marjorie (1985a). *The Dance of the Intellect: Studies in the Poetry of the Pound Tradition.* Cambridge: Cambridge UP, 1985.
Perloff, Marjorie (1985b). "'Letter, penstroke, paperspace': Pound and Joyce as co-respondents" in Perloff (1985a): 74-87.
Perloff, Marjorie (1985c). "Post-modernism and the Impasse of Lyric" in Perloff (1985a): 172-200.
Perry, Sam (1975). "Maximus of Gloucester from Dogtown: Charles Olson Personal Locus" in Davey (1975): 204-210.
Pinney, Marguerite (1969). "Vancouver: Brian Fisher Bau-Xi Gallery March, 1969." *ARTSCANADA* 132-133: 42.
Pinney, Marguerite (1983). "Voices" in *Vancouver: Art and Artists:* 174-187.
Poole, Nancy Geddes (1984). *The Art of London: 1830-1980.* London, Ont.: Blackpool.
Portugés, Paul (1978). *The Visionary Poetics of Allen Ginsberg.* Santa Barbara: Ross-Erikson.
Powell, Nicholas (1977). *Travellers to Trieste: The History of the City.* London: Faber.
Quartermain, Peter (1977). "Romantic Offensive: TISH." *Canadian Literature* 75: 77-84.
Quartermain, Peter and Meredith Quartermain (1986). "George Bowering" in New (1986): 84-92.
Reid, Dennis (1969). *Greg Curnoe,* exh. catalogue 10th Biennale, Sao Paolo.
Ricou, Laurie (1980-81). "Never Cry Wolfe: Benjamin West's *The Death*

of Wolfe in *Prochain Episode* and *The Diviners.*" *Essays on Canadian Writing* 20: 171- 85.

Ricou, Laurie (1987). "Triptych." *Canadian Literature* 113-114: 4-6.

Rilke, Rainer Maria (1983). *Briefe über Cézanne*. Frankfurt: Insel.

Robert, Guy (1978). *La Peinture au Québec depuis ses origines*. Sainte-Adelè: Iconia.

Robida, Michel (1974). *Le Déjeuner de Trieste*. Paris: Juillard.

Rosand, David (1981). "Composition/Decomposition/Recomposition: Notes on the Fragmentary and Artistic Process" in Kritzman (1981): 17-30.

Saba, Umberto (1978). *Thirty-One Poems*. Trans. Felix Stefanile. New York: Elizabeth Press.

Sarduy, Severo (1973). Address to the Symposium Roman des Amériques. *Liberté* 15.90: 255-278.

Sarduy, Severo (1974). "El barrocco y el neobarrocco" in Moreno 167-84.

Scott, Chris (1980). "A Bum Rap for Poor George Vancouver." *Books in Canada* 9.9: 9.

Seitz, William (1961). *The Art of Assemblage*. New York: Museum of Modern Art.

Shadbolt, Doris (1970). "On the Evolution of John Chambers' Perceptual Realism." *ARTSCANADA* 148/149: 57-62.

Silcox, David P. (1983). "An Outside View" in *Vancouver: Art and Artists*: 153-159.

Smith, D. Newton (1974). "The Influence of Music on the Black Mountain Poets, Part #1." *St. Andrews Review* 3: 99-115.

Smith, D. Newton (1975). "The Influence of Music on the Black Mountain Poets, Part #2." *St. Andrews Review* 3: 73-81.

Spanos, William V. (1972). "The Detective and the Boundary: Some Notes on the Post-modern Literary Imagination." *Boundary* 2 1.1: 147-68.

Statements: 18 Canadian Artists (1967). Regina: Norman Mackenzie Art Gallery.

Stevenson, Lionel (1939). *Dr. Quicksilver: The Life of Charles Lever*. London: Chapman.

Szylinger, Irene (1982). "Guido Molinari: at Yaslow/Salzman Gallery." *Arts Magazine*: n.p.

Tallman, Warren (1961). "'When a New Music is Heard the Walls of the City Tremble': A Note on Voice Poetry" in Davey (1975): 67-68.

Tallman, Warren (1972). "Wonder Merchants: Modernist Poetry in Vancouver during the 1960s" in Gervais (1976): 27-69.

Théberge, Paul (1976). *Guido Molinari* exh. catalogue. Ottawa: National Gallery of Canada.

Théberge, Paul (1982). *Greg Curnoe* exh. catalogue. Ottawa: National Gallery of Canada.

Thériault, Normand (1970). "New York a-t-il copié Montréal?" *La Presse* 3 octobre: C14.

Thomas, Alan (1981-82). "Photography of the Indian: Concept and Practice on the Northwest Coast." *B.C. Studies* 52: 61-85.

Valdès, Mario, ed. (1985). *Inter-American Literary Relationships.* New York: Garland.

Vancouver: Art and Artists 1931-1983 (1983). Vancouver: Vancouver Art Gallery.

Walser, Martin (1970). "Über die Neueste Stimmung im Westen." *Kursbuch* 20: 19-41.

Welsh, Robert (1978). "Molinari and the Science of Colour and Line." *RACAR* 5.1: 3-20.

Watson, Sheila (1982). "Preface" in Bowering (1982): 7-9.

Weatherhead, A.K. (1975). "Robert Duncan and the Lyric." *Contemporary Literature* 16.2: 163-174.

Weaver, Mike (1971). *William Carlos Williams: The American Background.* Cambridge: Cambridge UP.

Whalen, Terry (1988). "Discourse and Method: Narrative Strategy in George Bowering's *West Window.*" *Canadian Poetry* 22: 32-39.

Whitman, Walt (1855). *Leaves of Grass,* facsimile edition. New York: Columbia UP 1939.

Joyce Wieland (1987) exh. catalogue. Toronto: Art Gallery of Ontario.

Williams, William Carlos (1969). *Selected Essays.* New York: New Directions.

Wilson, Milton (1964). Rev. of *Points on the Grid. University of Toronto Quarterly* 34: 362-64.

Woodman, Ross (1967). "London (Ont.): A New Regionalism." *ARTSCANADA* 112/113: n.p.

Woodman, Ross (1980). "Jack Chambers as Film Maker." *Jack Chambers: The Last Decade:* 47-64.

Index

Abstract Expressionism 11
Acorn, Milton 24
Albers, Joseph 119
Allen, Donald 19
Alphabet: A Semiannual Devoted to the Iconography of the Imagination 51, 53
Aquin, Hubert 63
Aragon, Louis 55
Art and Correspondence 16
"Art becomes Reality" 18
ARTSCANADA 14, 53
Atwood, Margaret 10, 29, 56, 118
Avison, Margaret 19, 30, 121

Balkind, Alvin 13, 14, 18
Barbeau, Marcel 71
baroque 85
Barthes, Roland 116
Baxter, Iain 15, 17
Baxter, Ingrid 15
Bazlen, Roberto "Bobi" 99
Beaulieu, Michel 86
Beaulieu, Victor-Lévy 84, 85-88, 90-93
Bennett, W.A.C. 62
Berger, John 12, 98, 99, 101, 102, 110
Bergeron, Léandre 63
Bersianik, Louky 87
bissett, bill 15, 18

Black Mountain College 32, 86, 118-119
Blaser, Robin 10, 115
Borduas, Paul-Émile 71, 72
Borges, Jorge Luis 85
Bowering, Angela 29, 56
Bowering, George
 Allophanes 11, 75, 77, 84, 86, 115, 116
 Another Mouth 9, 42, 43, 54, 114, 120, 121
 Autobiology 54, 64-70, 74, 75, 113, 115
 "Breaking Up, Breaking Out" 29-30, 31, 33
 Burning Water 10, 12, 55, 64, 84, 86-93, 99, 102, 103, 105, 109, 110, 112, 115, 117, 118, 119
 Caprice 10, 84, 94, 103-111, 112, 115, 116, 117
 Concentric Circles 43
 The Concrete Island: Montreal Poems 1967-71 114
 "Confessions of a Failed American" 14
 Craft Slices 71, 87, 115, 116, 121, 122
 "the crumbling wall" 44
 "Dance to a Measure" 32, 42
 "Delsing" 116
 Errata 112, 114, 115

The Gangs of Kosmos 29, 38, 42
Genève 74, 115
"geopolitic" 41
"George, Vancouver" 61
George, Vancouver: A Discovery Poem 49, 87, 115
"A Great Northward Darkness: The Attack On History in Recent Canadian Fiction" 103
Harry's Fragments 112
"history is us" 46, 47-48
How I Hear "Howl" 26
In The Flesh 74, 75, 115
"Inside the Tulip" 31, 68, 83
Kerrisdale Elegies 10, 11, 12, 25, 54, 75-83, 99, 107, 113, 115, 117
Layers 1-13 54
Letters from Geeksville: RedLane to George Bowering, 1960-64 25
"L.S." (= "Locus Solus") 21
The Man in Yellow Boots / El hombre de las botas amarillas 12, 19, 27-39, 41, 42, 43, 44, 114
"the mark" 49
The Mask in Place 84, 115, 116
"Metaphor 1" 22, 31, 77
Mirror on the Floor 11, 13, 26, 41, 87, 112, 113, 116
"Modernism Could Not Last Forever" 44, 84
"Montreal" 71
"On a Black Painting by Tamayo" 11, 28, 33
"the plain" 41
"Points on the Grid" 23
"A Preface" 120
Protective Footwear 10, 65, 115, 120
"Reaney's Region" 49
Rocky Mountain Foot: a lyric, a memoir 25, 27, 40-50, 56, 115
Seventy-One Poems for People 50, 51, 71
A Short Sad Book 10, 54, 56-60, 62-64, 87, 115
The Silver Wire 27, 28, 31, 32, 42, 55, 114, 120
"Sir George Computer University" 71
"Spans" 10
"Stab" 74
Sticks and Stones 11, 114
"The Swing" 11, 32-33
"The Three-Sided Room: Notes on the Limitations of Modernist Realism" 84
Uncle Louis 11, 54, 120
"Universal and Particular: an Enquiry into a Personal Esthetic" 21
"vancouver-courtenay-calgary" 45
West Window: The Selected Poetry of George Bowering 119
"when you run naked" 32
"Why James Reaney is a Better Poet" 49
Bowering, Thea 43, 65
Boyle, John 52, 58, 62
Breeze, Claude 36
Breton, André 55
Brodzky, Anne 53
Bromige, David 23
Brossard, Nicole 87

Cage, John 17, 32, 36, 119
Calgary 17, 27, 44, 46, 49
Call Me Ishmael 86
Canada Council 14, 52, 122
Canadian Literature 117

Index

Cartier-Bresson, Henri 110
Cassady, Neal 75
Cézanne, Paul 73, 82
Chambers, Jack 12, 52, 54, 61, 64-70
Changes 13
Christmas, Douglas 13
Coleridge, Samuel 20, 103
collage 11, 35-39, 41, 42, 43, 55, 61, 94, 102, 112
La Construction du réel 79
Corman, Cid 19
correspondence art, correspondence artists 16, 17, 24
Corso, Gregory 19
Craig, Eric 16
Craig, Kate 16
Creeley, Robert 19, 117, 119
cubism, cubist 29, 37, 102
Cunningham, Merce 17, 31, 32, 36, 119
Curnoe, Greg 9, 10, 11, 52-58, 60, 61, 62, 63, 64
Curnoe, Owen 51, 61

dadaism, dadaist 16, 38, 43, 55, 58
Daedalus 101, 102
Daniells, Roy 117-118
Davey, Frank 15, 19, 20, 21, 23, 25, 42, 56, 120
Dawson, Dave 21, 31
"The Death of General Wolfe" 63
"The Death of Montcalm" 63
Di Cicco, Pier Giorgio 114
Di Prima, Diane 19
Dorn, Edward 47
Dorval Mural 54, 55, 58, 61-62
Dos Passos, John 101
Dragland, Stan 110
Dublin 98, 101
Dudek, Louis 19, 55, 120

Dumont, Gabriel 59
Duncan, Robert 19, 20, 21, 25, 42, 117, 119

Edmonton Art Gallery 62
El Corno Emplumado 13, 24, 28, 38, 55
Elder, Bruce 65
Eluard, Paul 55
Emerson, Ralph Waldo 44
Emery, Tony 13
enjambment 33, 79, 120
Erdman, Jean 18
Erickson, Arthur 17

Faust 103
Favro, Murray 53
Ferlinghetti, Lawrence 19
Fiedler, Leslie 119
Findley, Timothy 63
Finnegans Wake 18, 91
Fisher, Brian 9, 10, 11, 12, 36, 82-83
Fowles, John 100
Frye, Northrop 49, 56
Fuller, Buckminster 17, 119

Gagnon, François 72, 73
Gauvreau, Claude 73
Ginsberg, Allen 19, 26, 32, 33, 42, 44, 75
Giono, Jean 92
del Giudice, Daniele 98-99
Goguen, Jean 71
Goodwin, Helen 15, 17
Group of Seven 60
Guggenheim Museum 18

Hall, Donald 19
Hard Edge 9, 71, 72, 79, 82
historical novel 84, 100, 112, 115

historical photography 12
Hogg, Bob 93, 114
Hogg, Thomas 114

Icarus 101, 102
Imago 20, 115
Impressionism 32
Intermedia 14, 17, 53
"International Poetry Incarnation" 19
Intuition 17
Isaacs, Avrom 55

jazz 25-26
Johnson, Ray 18
Johnston, George 53
Jones, LeRoy 19
Joyce, James 18, 91, 98, 101
Juneau, Denis 71

Kamboureli, Smaro 10, 113
Kael, Pauline 18
Kane, Paul 59
Kearns, Lionel 19
Kennedy, Garry Neill 14
Kerouac, Jack 19, 25, 75, 113
Kiyooka, Roy 9, 10, 11, 12, 13, 18-19, 24, 25, 35-39, 71, 76
Kline, Franz 11, 119
de Kooning, Willem 119
Knutson, Susan 90
Kroetsch, Robert 121
Künstlerroman 112

Lalonde, Michèle 60, 61
Lamb, W. Kaye 117
Lambert, Michel 52
Lane, Red 21, 23, 24, 25, 27, 75
Lapierre, Rene 86
Laurence, Margaret 63

Leduc, Fernand 72
Lee, Dennis 118
Lee-Nova, Gary 19
Levertov, Denise 19, 25
Lewis, Glenn 16
London Art Gallery 52, 53
London Art Museum 51
London, England 61, 89
London, Ontario 49, 50, 51, 52, 53, 61, 64, 65, 67, 71
Lord, Barry 58, 59-60
Lorrain, Claude 109
Los Angeles 14
lyric, lyricism 22, 27, 30, 34, 35, 42, 67, 68, 69, 76, 83, 114, 115, 116

McClung, Nellie 62
McFadden, David 24, 25, 53
MacLennan, Hugh 59
Maclow, Jackson 32
McLuhan, Marshall 17-18
"Margins Into Lines: A Relationship" 21
Marinetti, Filippo 102
Mathews, Robin 9, 15
The Maximus Poems 25, 42, 45
Melville, Herman 85-93, 103
mimétisme 72
modernism, modernist 23, 43, 84, 98, 120
Molinari, Guido 12, 71-75, 77-79, 81, 82
Mondragon, Sergio 27, 28
monotype (improvisation) 37
montage 35
Montale, Eugenio 99
Montreal 13, 15, 36, 49, 55, 59, 71, 72, 73, 114
Morris, Michael 16, 17, 18
mural 52, 61, 62-63

Index

Museum of Modern Art (N.Y.) 37
Musil, Robert 101

National Gallery of Canada 52, 55, 62
Neil, Al 13, 17
neo-dadaism, see dadaism, dadaist 37, 55
Neo-Plasticiens 71, 72
New York 14, 55, 72, 101
Newman, Barnett 71
Nichol, bp 18, 43, 121
"Nihilist Spasm Band" 53
Norman Mackenzie Art Gallery 82

official art 60, 62, 101
O'Keeffe, Georgia 31
Olson, Charles 18, 19, 21, 25, 32, 42, 43, 45, 86, 94, 117, 119
Onley, Tony 18
Ortiz, Ralph 16, 17

Pack, Robert 19
Pachter, Charles 29
parataxis 69, 82, 98
Payne, Gordon 11
Perry, Sam 17, 45, 75
Pfeiffer, Bodo 36
Piaget, Jean 72, 79-80
Pop Art 9, 18
post-modernism, post-modernist 84-87, 92, 117
Pound, Ezra 24
projective verse 26, 32
Purdy, Al 24

Quartermain, Meredith 115
Quartermain, Peter 20, 115, 118

Randall, Margaret 24, 27, 28

Rauschenberg, Robert 17, 36, 119
Ray, Man 38, 113
Rayner, Gordon 55
realism 62, 85, 94, 100, 108, 111
Reaney, James 49, 51, 53, 60
Regina 82
Region Gallery 53
regionalism 9, 49-50, 52
Reid, Jamie 19
Riel, Louis 59
Rilke, Rainier Maria 77, 82, 98, 99, 103
Riopelle, Jean-Paul 71
Rivera, Diego 61
Robbe-Grillet, Alain 98, 100
Roberts, Charles G.D. 59
Rogatnick, Abraham 13, 17, 18
romanticism, romantics 20-21, 23
Rubens, Peter Paul 101

Saba, Umberto 98, 99
Saint-Martin, Fernande 79
San Francisco 14, 18, 19
Sanouillet, Michel 52, 55
Scobie, Stephen 18
Shadbolt, Doris 13, 18
Sheeler, Charles 113
Shelley, Percy Bysshe 26, 44, 49, 114
Silcox, David 14
Simpson, Louis 19
Sir George Williams University 28, 36, 49, 71
Skelton, Robin 18
Snow, Michael 52, 55
Sound Gallery, see Perry, Sam 17
Souster, Raymond 120
Steele, Bob 18
Stein, Gertrude 68, 74, 102, 111
Stern, Gerd 18
Svevo, Italo 93, 98, 99, 100, 102

surrealism 68, 73
de Swaan, Sylvia 29
Swift Current 20

Tallman, Warren 13, 15, 19, 26, 32, 117
Tanabe, Takao 18
terza rima 66
Théberge, Paul 55
Thomson, Tom 36, 63, 64
TISH 14, 15, 19-26, 27, 31, 35, 42, 45, 86, 114, 118, 119, 120, 121, 122
Toronto 13, 52, 60, 62
Tousignant, Claude 71, 72
Trasov, Vincent 16
Trieste 89, 93-103, 114
20/20 Gallery 53
Tzara, Tristan 55

University of British Columbia Festival of Contemporary Arts (UBC) 17, 18, 19
Fine Arts Gallery (UBC) 13, 18
Urquhart, Tony 59, 61

Vancouver 13-15, 17, 19, 21, 22, 27, 36, 46, 49, 52, 53, 71, 82, 99, 101, 119

Vancouver Art Gallery 13, 15, 17
Vancouver Poetry Festival 18
Vancouver School of Art 13-14, 19, 36
variable foot 26, 32
Vigneault, Gilles 58

Wah, Fred 19, 20, 21, 31
Washington 14, 60
Washington Gallery of Modern Art 71
Watson, Sheila 110, 112, 119
Watts, Alan 17
Webb, Phyllis 105
West, Benjamin 63, 101
Western Front Gallery 15
Whalen, Philip 19
Whitman, Walt 26, 42, 44, 113
Wieland, Joyce 52, 55, 56
Williams, William Carlos 19, 21, 25, 27, 31, 32, 34, 42, 43, 45, 105, 113, 120
Woodman, Ross 51, 66
Wordsworth, William 20

Yoko, Ono 18